PURCHASING
IN
GOVERNMENT

Forthcoming titles in the public sector management series

Accruals accounting in the public sector by V. Archibald
Managing change in the new public sector by R. Lovell
Strategic management and planning in the public sector by R. Smith
Marketing in the new public sector by L. Titman

Purchasing in Government

by
Patrick Behan

Published by Longman in association with

The Civil Service College.

PURCHASING IN GOVERNMENT

Published by Longman Information and Reference, Longman Group Limited, 6th Floor, Westgate House, The High, Harlow Essex CM20 1YR, England and Associated Companies throughout the world.

A catalogue record for this book is available from The British Library.

ISBN 0-582-23896-X

Contents

Series foreword

The Longman/Civil Service College series of texts on Management in the Public Sector covers many of the most important topics on the current management agenda, in central Government and in the public sector as a whole. In the past many of these topics may have been the preserve of specialists. Finance was for Finance Division, human resource issues were for the Personnel Group, contracts were for Contracts Branch. Increasingly all managers, at senior, middle and junior management levels, find themselves drawn into these, previously specialist, topics. With flatter management structures and increased delegation, all managers need a broad understanding of a range of management topics. This series of books has been produced with their needs in mind.

The texts are intended to be straightforward to understand, to provide a good summary of current understanding and best practice, and to illustrate the key points with examples from the public sector. There will still be room for the specialist, but these texts should enable every manager to talk intelligently with the specialist and understand him or her better.

At one time, in many Government departments, purchasing was something which could be left to anyone. The need for professionalism was then recognised and in recent years there has been a great deal of emphasis on building up professional purchasing groups, staffed by people with formal qualifications. However, with the growth of market testing, compulsory competitive tendering and contracting out, purchasing is now a subject of which virtually every middle and senior manager needs to be aware. This book is designed to provide that awareness.

Robert J. Smith

August 1994

Author's foreword

The need for effective Government purchasing has always been great, but no more so than in the present day, when strict budget control requires better value from every pound of taxpayer's money spent.

Great changes have taken place in many areas of Government purchasing over the last ten years. The critical role of the purchasing function is now more widely recognised and a strategic approach more commonly adopted. Both of these factors support the increasing development of a two-way interface with corporate management, greatly increasing the motivation at managerial and operational levels and ensuring that the impact of better purchasing in each department is more widely recognised and valued.

The introduction of Government policies concerning compulsory competitive tendering in local government and market testing in central Government has led to ever greater numbers of the general public and Government employees becoming more conscious of the terms 'purchasing' and 'contract'.

I have therefore written this book with two aims in mind. The first is to give the reader with little or no purchasing knowledge in either the Government or private sector a view of the purchasing function in Government. If it is read thoroughly, it will provide more than a basic understanding of some of the principles and practices of purchasing in general and Government purchasing in particular.

The second aim will be met if it is read more lightly, as it will provide an overview of Government purchasing of which, because of its ever increasing importance, all senior and middle managers should be aware.

Purchasing is such a wide subject that it is impossible to cover all aspects of the function in a single book of modest dimensions. I have been very selective, therefore, and have aimed to give an interesting flavour of some of the most important areas. Those who wish to pursue the topics further will find that many books have been written on most of the chapter headings.

I would like to thank Kerry Johnston, Alison Graham and Bob Pike for their work in producing the printed text.

> There is hardly anything in the world that some man cannot make a little worse and sell
> a little cheaper, and the people who consider price only are this man's lawful prey.
>
> (Attributed to John Ruskin 1819-1900, but not found in his works).

Patrick Behan
Sunningdale

Chapter 1

The critical role of purchasing

Government departments, just like any private sector concern, need to buy goods and services to conduct their business. The purchasing organisations within each department are of central importance in obtaining those goods and services, from both internal and external sources of supply.

Importance of purchasing

It is important to recognise from the outset that a good purchasing organisation contributes to profitability by helping both to reduce costs and to improve the effectiveness of production.

❑ Cost savings and the multiplier

In the *private* sector, where profitability is a leading motivator, the critical role of purchasing is often demonstrated along the lines of Figure1.1. This illustrates the 'multiplier' effect; a small improvement in the effectiveness of purchasing can have a large impact on the profitability of a business. Figure 1.1 shows the break-down of £100 million of sales revenue in a typical manufacturing business. In this situation a 2 per cent saving on purchases, made by a better-than-average purchasing organisation, would save £1 million, which translates into a 10 per cent increase in the level of profit, a multiplier effect of 5:1.

Of course it is possible for this business to increase its profitability by means other than improving the effectiveness of purchasing. However, such improvements may be less readily achieved. For example, the numbers in Figure 1.1 imply a return on sales of 10 per cent, (a profit of £10 million on turnover from £100 million.) If this margin is maintained it will take an increase in sales revenue of £10 million to produce an extra £1 million profit, ie a 10 per cent increase in sales would produce a 10 per cent increase in profitability. The multiplier effect of sales effort in this company is therefore 1:1 compared to a purchasing multiplier of 5:1.

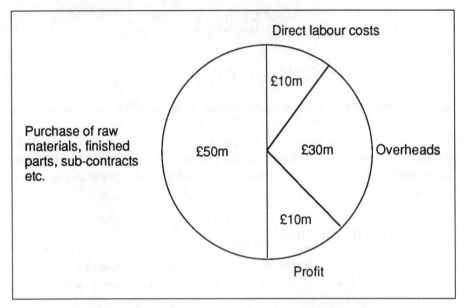

Figure 1.1 Total sales revenue of a typical manufacturing business

❑ Effectiveness of production and customer satisfaction

The above argument is valid but, in the wrong hands, can be a little dangerous, as it places too much emphasis on the role of the purchasing organisation to achieve *savings* by spending less. That is only one side of the purchasing coin. In the example above, a crude purchasing organisation might see their role solely in terms of making savings, as their way of contributing towards the profitability of the business. This could lead, for example, to the dubious practice of frequently changing suppliers in order to buy at the lowest price obtainable, driving the price down and down as an end in itself. Ultimately, something will crack, be it:

- excessive quality failures of the goods or services purchased
- unacceptably late deliveries
- total failure of the supplier to complete the work.

Even in small doses, such failures can have a detrimental effect on the sales revenue of the company. Instead of contributing towards profitability, the activities of the crude purchasing organisation may lead to the company's eventual demise as fewer and fewer customers are prepared to buy its uncertain output. The *prices* paid by the purchasing organisation may have been low but the *cost* to the company was enormous.

The real skill in purchasing effectively is to contribute to the profitability of the business by spending less and getting 'more'. 'More' may relate:

- simply to an increase in quantity
- to an improvement in quality
- to an improved method of obtaining the materials and services such that more efficient manufacture is achieved.

The opportunities for spending less and getting more are limited only by a purchaser's professional knowledge, negotiating skills, imagination and motivation.

❏ The contribution of effective purchasing in Government

Where does this view of purchasing take us when we know that Government departments do not exist to make a profit? In the private sector there is a ceiling to the price which a commercial business can charge for its output, thereby limiting the amount available for expenditure on purchased goods and services. Similarly there is a limit to the amount that Government can realistically spend to conduct its business. This limit is governed by:

- the level of borrowing deemed prudent by Government
- the level of direct and indirect taxes which the population will bear in return for the public services provided.

The importance of professional purchasing in Government has never been greater. The expectation of the citizen for more and better public services has come at a time when lower levels of employment have resulted in reduced tax revenues and when the public sector is borrowing £700 million a week.

This is not unlike the situation faced by any business striving for success in a highly competitive environment. The pro-active purchasing organisation seeks more from its suppliers for less money to enable the business to pass on more for less money to its customers.

❏ Public procurement policy

Government purchasing practices in this highly competitive world market need to match those of the best and most demanding private sector purchasing organisations. Central Government spent around £30 billion on goods and services in 1993, itself representing 4 per cent of Gross Domestic Product. Pro-active purchasing on this scale can positively influence the competitiveness of government suppliers and, with due regard to the EC Procurement Directives, the economy as a whole. Poor Government purchasing, on the other hand, could encourage uncompetitive practices in those parts of the economy where the public sector is a significant customer, leading to difficulties in selling to a world market. It should be no surprise, therefore, that it is the Government's policy that public sector purchasing staff should use the influence their purchases give them to help develop the competitiveness of their suppliers.

Government purchasing: general principles

The following principles of purchasing have been summarised from *Government Accounting*, (HM Treasury, 1991):

- purchasing should be based on value for money
- goods and services should be acquired by competition, unless there are convincing reasons to the contrary
- requirements which are above a certain threshold are normally required to be advertised in accordance with EC and GATT rules on public procurement
- there should be a clear definition of the roles and responsibilities of staff involved in specifying the need, giving financial authority and making purchasing commitments
- there should be separation of the financial authority and the purchasing authority
- there should be a separation of duties between staff who make contracts, those who receive the goods and those who authorise payment.

❏ Value for money criteria

It is still widely believed that central Government purchases are based upon lowest price alone. However, 'value for money' is the basis on which purchases should be made. In order to make value for money judgements during the purchasing process, clear criteria are required. The factors below are summarised from the *Public Purchasing Policy Guidelines* published by the Treasury in 1981. They are just as relevant today.

1 Status of firms involved

- financial viability; design capability; production capacity
- quality assurance status and track record; delivery record
- cost management arrangements and track record.

2 Equipment/services offered

- extent to which it meets the **minimum** requirement

- design/artistic qualities (where appropriate)

- compatibility with equipment already in use

- 'extras' above minimum requirement which offer cost effective advantage

- scope for improvement at a later date

- conformity with quality standards

- proven reliability; maintainability

- repair and servicing arrangements.

3 Immediate cost of acquisition

- initial price

- pricing arrangement eg firm price, fixed price, etc

- basis for agreeing prices on associated or follow-on orders

- payment terms (on delivery or stage payments)

- cost of financing stage payments

- transport costs; installation costs.

4 Delivery

- conformity with requirement; reliability of offer

- operational and financial effects of earlier/later delivery.

5 Operating costs

- running costs; cost of spares (present and future)

- servicing and maintenance costs; other support costs.

6 Product support

- quality of after sales facilities

- availability of spares (present and future).

7 Replacement arrangements

– receipts from eventual disposal; replacement timeframe.

8 Strategic and structural

– effect of current purchase on the price, availability and competition of future supplies.

Clearly, nearly all purchasing decisions are based upon a balance and judgement of many factors, only one of which is the price. The real value for money question is,

how much will the item purchased cost the department to own and use?

It is NOT,

what is the price?

Asking and answering the first question will ensure that every purchase achieves the greatest value from each pound of public money spent.

❏ Objectives

The main reason for the existence of any purchasing organisation is to provide the business with the products and services to meet corporate objectives. But the nature of government procurement is such that it is concerned not only with the end result but also with the way in which that result is achieved.

There are four main objectives of Government purchasing. These are:

(i) to provide end users with what they *need*, when they need it and at the best value for money

(ii) to provide Accounting Officers, and through them Parliament and the taxpayer, with value for money through expenditure on procurement

(iii) to protect the Accounting Officer's interests in procurement, by means of appropriate managerial and contractual arrangements

(iv) to contribute to the corporate management of a department.

This book examines how these objectives may be met by considering:

- the approach to *organising the purchasing function* for greater efficiency and effectiveness
- the *legal aspects of purchasing* and their effect on purchasing systems and procedures
- the contribution of effective *sourcing and supplier appraisal* towards value for money
- different *types of contract* and methods of *determining the price*
- the vital role of the *specification* in the purchasing process
- the importance of ensuring that appropriate *terms and conditions* of contract protect the department's interests
- what is meant by contractors rate of *profit* and how this might need to be assessed for certain types of government contract
- the value for money improvements that may be achieved through *negotiation*
- the effect of the *EC Supplies and Services Directives* on government purchasing.

References

HM Treasury (1991) *Government Accounting, Amendment No 3* London, HM Treasury

HM Treasury (1981) *Public Purchasing Policy Guidelines* London, HM Treasury

Chapter 2

Organising for effective purchasing

In this chapter we will consider the role of planning and control within procurement organisations and their implications for the structure of the organisation. Systems which have inputs and outputs, whether pieces of electronic equipment, some electro-mechanical hardware or a business organisation, all need to be controlled if they are consistently to produce the outputs for which they were designed. Without control, systems are apt to run away on their own and do what *they* want to do without any thought for their real purpose. Placing this in a Government procurement context, without proper control purchases may be made with little thought for the objectives of the purchasing organisation and of the Government department in whose name it is acting. If a good purchasing system is one that is properly controlled the starting point must be to:

- know what is to be achieved and set objectives
- measure the output against those objectives
- be able to correct undesirable outputs to maintain those objectives.

Complete control only exists when it is possible to predict the effects of the corrective action we may take to modify the processes. Without this predictive capability, corrective action can only be taken on a trial and error basis.

Procurement strategy, management and control system

In 1965, Robert Anthony developed a planning and control framework which defined three levels of control for any type of organisation. These were:

- strategic control
- management control
- operational control.

By considering that framework in a procurement context, it is possible to illustrate an outline organisational structure which should help to meet the planning and control needs.

❏ Definitions

Strategic planning is the process of:

- setting the objectives of the organisation
- deciding upon the resources to be used to achieve those objectives
- forming the policies used to govern the procurement, employment and disposition of those resources.

Strategic planning in purchasing is perhaps a rarer activity than it should be. It may be worth asking whether this is because the resources required to carry it through are frequently exhausted in reacting to day-to-day contractual problems and other procurement issues, issues which should ideally be resolved by trained, well-motivated staff at managerial and operational levels.

Management control is the means by which management ensures:

- that the resources required to execute the strategic plan are available
- that the resources are used efficiently and effectively to meet the department's objectives.

Operational control is the process of ensuring that particular tasks are carried out efficiently and effectively and is mainly concerned with the short-term activities of the organisation's operations.

A systematic approach to procurement requires action, therefore, at three different levels in the procurement organisation, namely:

- a strategic level
- a managerial level
- an operational level.

In addition, very short-term activities of an administrative nature may require a fourth and final level,

- an administrative level.

❏ Procurement activities and control levels

Procurement activities will now be divided broadly between the four main categories suggested immediately above.

Strategic activities

Strategic activities in procurement are concerned with setting the framework of operation and providing a two-way interface with corporate management. They include:

- planning and developing the procurement role and infrastructure
- setting and maintaining procurement policy
- setting the operational standards to be achieved
- targeting expertise and resources for best effect
- establishing control and reporting systems
- providing budget planning advice.

Managerial activities

Managerial activities focus upon the efficient and effective use of resources in meeting the organisation's strategic procurement objectives. This requires that control and reporting procedures exist to ensure, for example, the following:

- compliance with EC/GATT and other government purchasing policies
- that products and services are suitably specified
- that supplier performance is satisfactory
- that the significant buying power of the department is exploited
- that stockholding costs and administration costs are minimised
- that market knowledge is used to aid budget planning
- that major procurements are properly managed
- that the purchasing organisation is efficient
- that the risk of impropriety is minimised.

Operational activities

Operational activities cover the day-to-day tasks that are readily recognised by all and sundry as purchasing activities. Examples are meeting with suppliers' representatives, inviting tenders, placing contracts, negotiating prices, dealing with specific contractual problems, and so on.

Administrative activities

Although administrative activities are the routine tasks of a short-term nature, they can be vital to the effective operation of the purchasing function. They cover such tasks as record keeping and updating previous purchases, previous prices and the method of purchase, the careful maintenance of contract files, the pursuance of acceptance documents and acknowledgement letters.

Organisational models for purchasing

Before further considering the four levels of planning and control, it is worthwhile to examine some common organisational models for the purchasing function.

❑ Centralisation v decentralisation of purchasing

In both the public and private sectors, the extent to which purchasing activities should be centralised continues to be debated. Some firms and smaller Government departments centralise these activities almost completely, with all buying carried out at a central headquarters. Others entirely decentralise the function, with each part of the business having full power to conduct its purchasing activities. Almost inevitably the majority of organisations lie somewhere between these two extremes, within both the private and the public sectors. Some of the benefits of each approach will now be considered. Generally speaking, the advantage of one is the disadvantage of the other.

Advantages of centralised purchasing

The advantages of centralised purchasing may be summarised as:

- aggregation of requirements
- increased purchasing expertise
- more effective coordination and control.

First, consider aggregation of requirements. Larger, consolidated purchase requirements should be an outcome of centralised purchasing. Because they are more attractive to potential suppliers, such increased quantities permit the negotiation of better supplier performance and more favourable prices than purchasing piecemeal. In addition, the administrative cost saving from managing a smaller number of larger contracts can be significant.

Secondly, there is no doubt that the centralisation of purchasing greatly contributes towards the development of more skilled and knowledgeable purchasing staff, leading to greater expertise and technical understanding on the part of the buyers involved. In most departments, the complex nature of the products and services procured means that buying staff need a certain level of technical competence. Without this, they and their associated purchasing activities are perceived as having little more than a clerical status and the function is invariably exiled to that level as more and more important purchasing decisions are made by the users.

Thirdly, centralised purchasing permits more direct control at the strategic, managerial and operational levels. Important policy decisions such as those concerning the use of certain types of contract, EC procurement methods, consistency of contract terms and conditions, and purchasing ethics, are generally easier to deliver at all levels within the function.

Conversely, the decentralisation of purchasing can lead to a situation where there is little or no control. Adhoc arrangements abound and, because there is no appreciation of the overall value of the buying department's purchases, in either the buyers' or the sellers' eyes, deals are struck which miss many value for money opportunities. Ultimately, if all control is lost, decentralisation will feed on itself such that everyone in the organisation will become a 'purchaser', and once this climate has developed it is very difficult to change.

Advantages of decentralisation

The advantages of decentralised purchasing may be summarised as:

- ease of communication and speed of operation
- autonomy of budget holders.

Users of highly centralised purchasing functions are often vociferous about the difficulties they encounter when attempting to achieve a rapid response to their requisitions and contractual queries. Centralisation not only causes a physical delay of two or three days when using normal methods of communication, but it also acts as a buffer to users' attempts to seek help with a specific problem or to ascertain the cause of a particular delay. The homogeneous mass presented by a fully centralised purchasing organisation to anyone outside is a real barrier to effective communication and to meeting the users' needs. This tends to lead to frustration on the part of the user and may provoke the development of dubious practices by the user to avoid becoming entangled with the centralised function.

Generally, decentralised purchasing, with purchasing officers close to the person wanting the supplies, allows quicker, more direct communication, and facilitates the development of sound working relationships between the purchasers and the users. However, because these relationships develop, there is a risk that purchasing staff who are not fully committed to the purchasing organisation might lose sight of their higher level objectives when faced with pressure to meet individuals' short-term needs. Without the powerful monitoring and support of a centralised function on policy matters, standards can rapidly decline.

Turning to the question of autonomy of budget holders, there has been a large increase in the number of budget holders in government as a result of greater delegation of financial responsibility. Inevitably such budget holders look for and expect full authority over expenditure, so as to match their responsibility. At the extreme, full decentralisation of purchasing could leave full authority with individual budget holders. In such situations there is a danger that many of the potential benefits of proactive purchasing are missed, if any purchasing function which remains is seen by the budget holders as no more than a purely mechanistic processor of their requirements.

It can be argued that budget holders can ultimately exercise control even if purchasing is strongly centralised, in that it is generally possible for budget holders to establish a framework within which indirect control can be exercised over the performance of the purchasing function. If that is accepted, the main area of difficulty when purchasing is fully centralised is that of effective communication, as described earlier, rather than control itself.

A mixture of centralised and decentralised control

A mix of centralised and decentralised control would normally take the form of central responsibility for policy making and high value purchases, with decentralised responsibility for low value purchases. The centralised procurement policy department would then plan and control at the strategic level. Similarly, high value, high risk purchases are likely to be more efficiently and effectively managed by specialised, highly skilled purchasing staff at the centre. Low value, low risk purchases tend to be more routine by nature and so can generally be controlled on an operational and administrative level alone.

This is a popular approach to attempt to gain the benefits of centralised purchasing on procurement policy matters and high value, high risk purchases, while retaining for low value, low risk purchases the flexibility and speed of response that decentralised purchasing provides.

The link between the type of organisation and the four levels of planning and control can now be seen as follows:

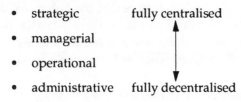

- strategic   fully centralised
- managerial
- operational
- administrative   fully decentralised

There is a natural tendency for strategic planning issues to stem from the centre of an organisation, from where corporate objectives and policy can extend to other parts of the function. A centralised view of the function, based upon accurate information from and discussions with the satellite operations, can help in the formulation of relevant and effective procurement policies.

There is a danger that, as an organisation becomes more decentralised, it will gradually lose its corporate identity and allegiance to corporate objectives such that, ultimately, its activities focus not on matters of policy but on day-to-day administrative expediences. In some very low value, very low risk situations, purchasing activities may successfully take place on an administrative level alone, but these situations will be rare.

Between the two extremes of fully centralised purchasing, the home of strategic planning, and fully decentralised purchasing, the short-term, administrative unit, is the organisational structure best able to help the function fully meet its high level objectives by focusing attention on those activities which are seen to be deficient. The exact nature of this structure and of the boundaries between centralisation and decentralisation should ultimately depend on the nature of the business and of the goods and services which it has to purchase.

❏ Organisation by product or service

Whether or not a centralised or decentralised approach to purchasing is taken, there remains the challenge of how to organise at the management, operational and administrative levels. Only the larger Government departments and private companies will support separate purchasing units for each major product or service purchased. Such units, which are responsible for a narrow, well-defined range of goods or services, frequently develop into small teams of motivated individuals who are experts in their particular field. One disadvantage of this unit approach is the duplication of buying effort that exists at the administrative level, and to some extent the operational level, depending upon the amount of overlap between the products and services bought by the purchasing units.

❏ Location of the purchasing function in an organisation

Whether the purchasing function is centralised, decentralised or a mixture of both, there remains the question:

to whom should the purchasing function report?

The structure of any organisation reflects the attitude of management towards the activities involved in each arm of operation. In government, managing and monitoring the budget has been seen as a high level, high profile, high powered activity. Until recent years, procurement and purchasing, how the budget was spent, have been seen in some departments as low level, low profile, low powered activities. The real meaning of procurement and the positive contribution which effective procurement can make to an organisation is gradually becoming increasingly recognised and realised. However, the position of purchasing in the organisation, in both the private and public sectors still varies a great deal from organisation to organisation.

In general terms, the purchasing function provides a service to its users and the organisation as a whole. Ultimately its position and influence will depend upon its ability to demonstrate consistently high performance, in the same way that it would expect from its suppliers, and to make a strategic contribution to the organisation.

Reference

R N Anthony (1965) *Planning and Control Systems: A Framework for Analysis* Boston, Mass. Harvard Business School

Chapter 3

The legal aspects of purchasing

A thorough understanding of the 'formation of contract', that is how and when a contract is made, is one of the keys to the achievement of a Government department's or public sector organisation's purchasing objectives. Central Government spends about £30bn per annum on goods and services. For each of the purchases involved, whether valued at £10 or £100m, a contractual relationship is formed between the Government buyer and the commercial seller.

At this point it is worth noting that the Crown can sue and be sued in contracts in the same way as any citizen or company. Some people still mistakenly believe that the Crown cannot be sued by one of its contractors. However, the Crown Proceedings Act of 1947 enables Government departments, or the Attorney General where there is no department, to be sued by the ordinary processes of law in cases where, previously, the petition of right procedure would have applied. Alleged infringement by a Government department of public procurement legislation relating to works, supply, service or utility contracts may lead to the issue of a writ in the High Court (or Court of Session in Scotland). Furthermore, under the EC Compliance Directive, aggrieved suppliers can take action against non-compliant Government departments in the courts of the United Kingdom.

If disputes over a contract reach the courts, it is usually necessary to determine the precise point, the time and the place, at which a contract was made. This has to be done in order to establish whose terms and conditions applied, so that the rights and obligations of the parties to the contract can be understood. If a Government department wishes to enforce a contract without resorting to court action, it will still need to know precisely when the contract was created, so as to be certain that the (appropriate) Government terms and conditions applied to protect the Accounting Officer's purchasing interests.

It is only natural that commercial sellers will want to achieve the best deal for their company. This means that, given the opportunity, they will enter contracts subject to *their* terms and condjtions, which will have been carefully formulated to maximise the commercial opportunities and minimise the commercial risk to the supplier. Under these terms of contract, any risks arising will be passed on to the buyer, and so become the responsibility of the purchasing department.

Committed Government purchasers will strive to achieve the best deal that meets *their department's* objectives and these will be (or should be) embodied in *the department's* terms and conditions. For example, some typical conditions might cover:

- the specification for the goods or services
- the rights of the department and the obligations of the supplier if the specification is not fully met
- the delivery or completion date
- the rights of the department and the obligations of the supplier if the delivery or completion date is not fully met
- the price (or pricing arrangement) and what it covers
- the type of price ie whether firm or subject to variation
- when payment will be made, in full after completion or in stages during the course of the contract
- when 'ownership' of the goods passes from the supplier to the department
- when 'risk' in the goods passes from the supplier to the department
- the right of the department to 'break' the contract and the obligations to the supplier if that right is invoked.

It is only from an understanding of *how* and *when* a contract is made that the Government purchaser can be reasonably sure that contracts will be made subject to the Government department's terms and conditions.

Definitions of contracts

A brief and commonly used definition of a contract is as follows:

> a contract is a legally binding agreement between two or more parties.

Under English law, there are several 'categories' of contract, but for most Government purchasing purposes only two need to be considered. These are:

- a 'contract by deed'
- a 'simple contract'.

❑ Contracts by deed (or under seal)

Many of us in our personal lives will have bought a house, perhaps on more than one occasion as we have moved from job to job. If our house purchase was in England or Wales, we probably remember signifying our full agreement to the written terms by signing a document which laid out the conditions of the deal. After the document was *signed* by both parties, it was then *sealed* with a red adhesive seal and finally the document was exchanged or *delivered* between the parties. These actions, to sign, to seal and to deliver the documents, form the basis of a contract by deed. In England and Wales, under the terms of the Law of Property Act (1925), contracts for house purchase or the transfer of land need to be made 'by deed', that is, the contract needs to be *in writing* and must be *'signed, sealed and delivered'*.

❑ Simple contracts

Very few public sector purchasing staff need to become involved with contracts under seal. This is because, under English and Scottish Law, goods and services may be bought by way of 'simple contracts'. Simple contracts do not need to be evidenced in writing, and they do not have to be signed, sealed or delivered.

In everyday life, simple contracts are the means by which people buy groceries, newspapers, cars, televisions, video recorders and so on. They are also the means by which purchasing staff buy computers, office furniture, armoured vehicles, window cleaning services, helicopters, stationery, printing, and more.

But what *are* the requirements of a simple contract if, unlike contracts by deed, they do not have to be signed, sealed and delivered?

❑ How to make a simple contract

Simple contracts may be made in THREE ways, namely:

   (i) expressly, *by word of mouth*

  (ii) expressly, *in writing*

 (iii) implied, *by the action of the parties*.

When out shopping, purchases are frequently made by conversing with the shop assistant, thereby making a simple contract by word of mouth. In such circumstances, rights and obligations are accrued by both parties. Either may need to enforce them once the contract has been made.

Similarly, in everyday life, it is not unusual for contracts to be implied by the action of the parties. For example, some multi-storey car parks involve taking a ticket at the entry barrier and making payment on exit. A contract would have been created, at some point, by each party's action. The purchase of a bar of chocolate from a vending machine is another example of a simple contract that is implied by the action of the parties.

19

So if it is perfectly 'legal' to make a simple contract that *is not* in writing, why should Government purchasing staff go to great lengths to make their department's contracts in writing? There are three main reasons. The written contract:

(i) provides a clear audit trail in the contract file, showing why, how and when, the department

- bought what it did
- chose that supplier
- arrived at the price, or pricing arrangement

(ii) provides written evidence of the contract should a dispute arise about, say, the delivery or the specification or the price or any other condition

(iii) forces the department to think carefully about its requirements before writing them down, thereby helping to protect the Accounting Officer's interests in the purchase, by means of appropriate contractual arrangements.

Although written contracts are the norm in public sector purchasing, it is important for the parties to the contract to remember that these simple contracts may be legally created and amended *by word of mouth*, for example, by telephone or face-to-face at meetings. There is, therefore, a risk of unwittingly committing a purchasing organisation during pre-contract negotiations or during meetings or discussions with a contractor or potential contractor.

Legal requirements of a simple contract

In order for a simple contract to exist, it is necessary, under English Law, for the following essential elements to be present:

(i) an *offer*
(ii) an *unqualified acceptance* of that offer
(iii) *consideration*
(iv) an *intention to create a legal relationship*
(v) the *capacity* of the parties to enter into a contractual relationship
(vi) the *lawfulness of the object* of the contract
(vii) *reality of consent.*

Although the list above may appear quite lengthy, from a practical point of view it is the first two, *offer* and *unqualified acceptance*, which cause most misunderstanding and difficulty in government purchasing.

❏ The offer

An offer, whether made by word of mouth, in writing or implied by conduct, may be defined as

a definite promise to be bound on certain specified terms.

Purchasing staff should be careful to distinguish between an 'offer' and something known as an 'invitation to treat'. An invitation to treat is a communication, to a person or group of persons, inviting them to make an offer to the party sending the invitation. For example, when a Government department wishes to meet one of its requirements by seeking competitive tenders it sends out an 'invitation to tender' to suitable suppliers. This invitation to tender is an invitation to treat, in that the Government department is asking the suppliers who have been approached to make the department an offer. In other words, the tenderers are asked to offer their price, delivery, and so on, to carry out work to the department's specification and terms and conditions contained in the tender documents.

In everyday life, we may see goods displayed in shop windows with a price label attached. Surprisingly, this does not represent an offer by the shop to sell those goods at that price to the general public. In fact it is merely an *invitation* from the shop to members of the buying public, for them to make an offer to the shopkeeper to purchase the goods in question. In other words, the window display is an invitation to treat. This matter was considered in a well-known case in 1961 *(Fisher v Bell)* when the defendant was prosecuted for offering for sale a flick-knife displayed in his shop window with a price tag attached. Under the Restriction of Offensive Weapons Act of 1959, it was illegal to *offer* such articles for sale. The successful defence was that the shop window display was NOT an offer for sale but an invitation to the buying public to make an offer ie an invitation to treat. As a result of this case, the Restriction of Offensive Weapons Act was amended to make it an offence even to display such items for sale.

Similarly, most advertisements for the supply of goods or services are *not* offers of sale *but* invitations to treat. They invite their readers (or viewers) to respond with an offer to purchase. The consequence of this is that suppliers' catalogues do not generally contain offers to provide goods or services at a particular price and delivery. Instead, they invite the purchaser to make the supplier an offer to buy. In practice, a Government department will, or should, offer to buy at the catalogue price (or less) but to its own terms and conditions.

This matter was considered by the courts in the case of *Partridge v Crittenden* (1968), whereby the defendant was prosecuted for *offering* for sale, by advertisement, a species of bird protected by law. His successful defence was that the advertisement was NOT an offer for sale BUT an *invitation* to the general public to respond with an offer to buy one of the birds.

It will be recognised from the points made so far that, in the course of their duties, public sector purchasing staff will find themselves *inviting offers* when going out to tender, and *making offers* when simply responding to a supplier's catalogue. Once the purchaser has *made* an offer *to* the supplier or the purchaser has *received* an offer *from* the supplier, an *unqualified acceptance* is ultimately required if a contract is to exist.

❏ The unqualified acceptance

An unqualified acceptance is an acceptance that corresponds to *all* the terms of the offer. Unless otherwise stated, the unqualified acceptance can be:

- made by word of mouth
- made in writing
- implied by the action of the parties.

Normally, if a Government department wishes to make a contract following a competitive tender, it needs only to signify its unqualified acceptance of the offer submitted by the successful tenderer for a contractual relationship to exist. This would generally be done in writing, using simply the words:

.... we hereby accept your tender ....

These words would form part of the tender acceptance letter, signed by the Purchasing Officer with the appropriate level of delegated authority from the Accounting Officer. Thus a contract will have been formed, (we will see precisely where and when later in this chapter). Figure 3.1 summarises the action taken by the parties to the contract in a straightforward single or competitive tender situation.

Very complex competitive tenders may not always be quite that straightforward, but the basic elements of offer and unqualified acceptance must be present for a contract to be formed in the tender process. In any event, it should be the Government department which makes its choice of the best supplier's offer, NOT the supplier choosing if it wishes to contract with the Government department!

Creating a contract through a tendering procedure for goods or services

Summary of key stages

1 Government department issues 'invitation to tender' documents containing the specification and terms and conditions to which any resulting contract will be subject. This is an *invitation to treat* inviting *offers* from the tenderers.

2 The tenderers respond to the invitation to tender by submitting their tender, that is, their *offer* in accordance with the specification and terms and conditions proposed.

3 The Government department evaluates the tenders (offers) submitted and makes an *unqualified acceptance* of the successful tender and rejects those that offer less value for money or that are non-compliant. A *contract* is created by the department's selection and unqualified acceptance of the winning offer.

Figure 3.1 Creating a contract

After the tender evaluation stage, some Government departments have issued documents to the successful tenderer which ask for *the supplier's* acceptance of the order for work. This approach can be disastrous! By offering the requirement back to the 'successful' tenderer, the department runs the risk that the supplier will accept with strings attached. For example, the supplier may say that the work will be done but that the price has now increased or that the supplier's conditions of contract will apply or that delivery will be later! In other words, the whole purpose of competitive tendering will have been lost. What should that department do now? Pay up? Re-tender, given that the unsuccessful tenderers have already had their tenders rejected? This is a messy situation which could have been avoided with a clearer understanding of a little contract law.

❑ Contracts without tendering

When a public sector organisation wishes to make a contract for the supply of, say, some very low value goods, use of a tendering procedure would be inappropriate, (see chapter 4). In this case, an 'order' for the goods, an *offer* to purchase at a certain price and to the purchaser's terms and conditions, would be sent to a supplier. For a contract to exist, the supplier is required to make an *unqualified acceptance* of the purchaser's *offer*.

To obtain this unqualified acceptance from the supplier, many purchasers send two copies of the order, asking that one be 'immediately' signed and returned by the supplier as the 'acceptance copy'. This is the wisest approach as it is possible in this way to ensure that contracts are made to the purchaser's terms and conditions, but it is not foolproof if the supplier used is not good administratively. In practice, 'immediately' may turn out to be *after* the goods have been delivered, if it is returned at all. In these circumstances, it is possible that the supplier has made an unqualified acceptance by his conduct, that is the act of delivering the goods ordered. However, if the goods are delivered along with a letter stating that the supplier's terms and conditions apply, then this is likely to be a *counter-offer* from the supplier rather than an unqualified acceptance. If the goods are then taken into use, the counter-offer is likely to have been accepted by the action of the department and a contract made which incorporates the supplier's terms and conditions. This is unlikely to be a satisfactory outcome from the purchaser's point of view should a contractual problem arise at a later stage.

A Government department or public sector organisation should normally adopt competitive tendering and therefore be looking to make an unqualified acceptance of the supplier's offer. Anything else is only tolerable for low value, low risk items. For requirements where competitive tendering is appropriate, the process outlined in Figure 3.1 ensures that it is the purchaser who is 'in control' and so forms the contract, when it chooses to do so, by making an unqualified acceptance of the best compliant tender.

❏ Post-tender negotiation

It is necessary to consider the situation where a purchaser may not be in a position to make an unqualified acceptance of a supplier's tender. Perhaps none of the bids is satisfactory as it stands, or it may be that the purchaser has chosen to carry out some post-tender negotiation, in order to seek an improved offer from one or more of the tenderers. If as a result of discussions or meetings any improvements or changes are made by the tenderers at this stage, it is important to record these changes as revised offers. The tenderers should, for record purposes, submit or confirm their revised offers in writing. In this way, the purchasing organisation remains 'in the driving seat', creating the contract when it chooses to do so, by the issue of an unqualified acceptance of the best (revised) offer made.

Communication of offers and acceptance

It has been seen *how* a contract is made, but not yet *where* and *when*. The *general rule* is that an offer, a revocation of an offer or an unqualified acceptance need to be communicated to the other party concerned. For example, if an offer were to be made either face-to-face or by telephone with another party, it would be deemed to have been communicated when it was *heard* (not when it was spoken). The same rule would apply to a revocation and an acceptance made face-to-face or by telephone. However, if *post* (Royal Mail) were used as the method of communication, the following Postal Rule applies (unless otherwise agreed between the parties):

(a) an offer would be deemed to have been communicated when it was delivered

(b) a revocation of an offer would be deemed to have been communicated when it was delivered, *but*

(c) an unqualified acceptance would be deemed to have been communicated *when it was posted* in the Royal Mail system, correctly addressed and stamped.

The consequence of this rule, which stems from a case in 1818 *(Adams v Lindsell)*, is that in a tender situation, the purchaser's unqualified acceptance of a tenderer's offer need not be received by the successful tenderer for a contract to exist. It is sufficient for the unqualified acceptance to have been posted for a contract to come into being. Although it is the posting of the purchaser's unqualified acceptance which creates the contract, giving reasonable certainty as to when and where the contract is made, it is good and usual practice to ask the contractor to confirm receipt of the contract documents sent with the tender acceptance letter. In this way, both parties have certain full knowledge of the existence of the contract.

❏ Need for signatures

Some Government departments go to great lengths to get two signatures on their contract documents, that of the department's representative and that of the contractor's. This practise is generally pointless and can be positively dangerous, (unless, of course, the contract is being made under seal, which is anyway unnecessary for the purchase of goods and services.) Simple contracts can be made in writing, by word of mouth or implied just from the action of the parties, so legal and enforceable contracts do not need any signatures. However, from a proof and audit point of view, a signature or two would be useful. But what is it desirable to sign? It is important that any tender received by the department is a genuine offer. The tenderer's signature on the tender document, with their position in the company, would normally indicate that this is the case. Once the purchaser's organisation has chosen the successful tenderer, it will wish to issue the acceptance letter mentioned earlier. This would be signed by the purchasing officer with the appropriate level of delegated authority. That is sufficient. The offer is signed by the tenderer and the unqualified acceptance of that offer is signed by the purchaser. Evidence of the contract exists in the contract file.

But what about some Government departments' perceived need for two signatures on the contract document, the buyer's and the supplier's? Apart from rarely serving any purpose, this practice can lead the purchaser into difficulties. To imply to the successful tenderer that a signature is required before a contract exists between the department and the supplier effectively hands over a significant amount of negotiating power to that tenderer. In this situation, the successful tenderer may say, for example:

> I will sign if you accept a higher price and my conditions concerning payment.

Now what? Negotiate or move on to the next best tender? Either of these options is a poor compromise, given that the department could have avoided the problem in the first place by forming the contract simply by an unqualified acceptance of the best tender.

❑ Call-off contracts and standing offers

As explained earlier, an invitation to tender is merely an invitation to treat, the tender itself amounting to the offer. However, in the public sector there can be various types of tender.

Where a purchaser invites tenders for the supply of specific goods (or services) on a specific date, the unqualified acceptance of the tender by the purchaser gives rise to a contract. Similarly, where a purchaser invites tenders for the supply of goods (or services) over a specific period of time, the acceptance of the tender gives rise to a contract. The fact that the goods (or services) are to be delivered (or completed) and payment is to be made by instalments does not affect the formation of the contractual relationship.

A different situation exists where a department invites tenders for the supply of goods or services of no definite amount 'as and when required.' Any tender thus submitted amounts to a *standing offer*, such that when the successful tenderer is sent a letter of acceptance, *no* contractual relationship is formed. In this case, acceptance takes place, and a contract is created, on each occasion when a 'demand' for a specific quantity of goods (or a particular service) is made. Each request for delivery of goods (or completion of a service) amounts to a separate acceptance, creating a series of contracts. Because the tender is a standing offer, the rules relating to offers apply, namely, *it may be revoked at any time* provided that it has not been accepted.

The special nature of standing offers was considered by the courts in 1873 in the case of *Great Northern Rail Co v Witham* in which the plaintiffs advertised for tenders for the supply of stores. The defendants submitted a tender in the following terms:

> We undertake to supply Great Northern Rail Co for 12 months with such quantities of goods as the company may order from time to time.

The company accepted the tender and subsequently issued various orders which were executed by the defendant. Ultimately, the company gave an order which the defendant refused to supply. The courts decided that the defendants were in breach of contract by refusing to make delivery. The tender was a standing offer which could be converted into a series of contracts, a separate contract each time the company accepted by making an order.

In Government contracting, such purchasing arrangements are common, though not widely understood. As stated above, the standing offer may be revoked at any time prior to its acceptance. This means that orders (acceptances) posted by the purchaser before the supplier's revocation of the standing offer is received by the purchaser are contractually binding. Subsequent orders will have no effect as the offer no longer exists.

This all means that a government purchaser may believe that a two or three year contract exists when, in fact, a series of contracts will be made over the period as each acceptance of the standing offer is made, as long as the supplier chooses not to withdraw the standing offer before the end of the period! To avoid this uncertainty, some government departments simply pay some consideration, for example £5, in return for the promise from the supplier NOT to withdraw their standing offer before the end of the period. (This action is not necessary under Scottish Law because a promise, such as to keep an offer open for a certain period, once accepted, is binding). Other departments go to the administrative extreme of drawing up a contract under seal.

All public sector purchasers and their managers should be aware of the term 'standing offer' and how it may be withdrawn at any time. They should not think that a contractual relationship exists from the initial acceptance of the supplier's standing offer. Neither should they believe that, if the contract duration says 3 years, this may only be changed if the contract terms and conditions allows. They should understand that the contract terms and conditions only relate to each of the series of contracts.

Chapter 4

Competitive tendering,

sourcing and supplier appraisal

In chapter 1, some examples of value for money criteria were listed, these being a selection of the typical factors that a professional purchasing organisation would take into account, according to the nature of each procurement, during the purchasing process. Value for money has been defined by the Treasury, in the context of purchasing, as:

> an 'economic' benefit generated by a purchaser's initiative and achieved by an action beyond that arising from mechanistic order placing.

Haggling over price and competitive tendering may both fit the definition of action beyond mechanistic order placing, but neither will, of its own, ensure value for money. If purchasing is viewed simply as a price haggling activity at the contract award stage, the outcome in the longer run is likely to be poorer value for money for the end-user and the taxpayer, as a result of too much emphasis on price at the expense of overall performance.

Competitive tendering

In a competitive tender situation, purchasers are simply making use of competitive market forces to obtain the best offer that the market is generating at that particular point in time.

❏ The prerequisites

As explained in chapter 1, competitive tendering is one of the principles underlying Government purchasing activities, as a contribution to seeking and demonstrating good value for money. From a purely purchasing point of view, certain prerequisites need to be satisfied before competitive tendering can be considered the appropriate method of procurement. These are:

- the specification of the product or service must be complete and clear, to both the purchasing organisation and the potential suppliers

- the market must be competitive, there should be a sufficient number of sellers who actively want to compete with one another for the work

- the value of the purchase must be sufficiently large to warrant this procedure as the administrative cost to both the buyer and the potential suppliers is high

- there must be sufficient time available for the process to be carried out effectively.

Absence of one or more of these prerequisites should not necessarily be seen as a legitimate reason for concluding that competitive tendering is impracticable. Indeed the response should normally be action to overcome the difficulty, so that the Government's procurement policies (and perhaps those of the Economic Community enacted under EC procurement legislation) are not breached.

It is also important for the buying organisation to remind itself repeatedly that the completed tender documents returned by each tenderer represent that supplier's offer which, if unconditionally accepted by the buyer, will form a legally binding agreement, the contract. The buyers should try to imagine themselves as the seller, faced with the tender documents to complete, knowing that promises made at this stage will, once accepted by the purchaser, become contractually binding. It is easy, then, to recognise that uncertainty on the part of the tenderers will increase their perception of the risk. This in turn will lead to fewer competitors for the requirement and larger cost contingencies within the price.

Therefore, a key principle of competitiveness is that as much certainty as possible should be provided to the tenderers to help them keep their business risks to a manageable level. This will encourage a more competitive market (and increase the buyer's choice) and keep the tenderer's contingency costs (faced by the purchaser) to a practical minimum.

This 'certainty' requires a clear understanding not only of the specification at the tender stage but also of the terms and conditions of any contract resulting from the tender process.

❏ The process

The objective of the competitive tendering process is to ensure that a contractual relationship is formed with the most suitable supplier in the market for the goods or services required. The most suitable supplier is the one who:

- is financially sound
- is technically and commercially capable of providing the goods or services required

- submits the best offer in value for money terms
- is likely to execute the contract efficiently and effectively based on their track record.

The competitive tendering process can be seen in the purchasing cycle shown in Figure 4.1.

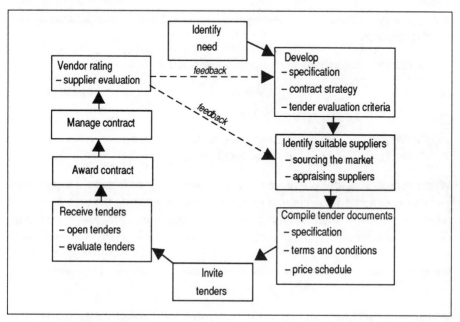

Figure 4.1 The purchasing cycle

Difficulties may arise if the purchasing function is not involved at the earliest opportunity, as they will be best able to advise or act upon such matters as:

- the commercial and legal aspects of the specification
- the evaluation of innovative proposals from tenderers
- sourcing the market and supplier appraisal
- the time required for the competitive tendering process
- the type of contract and pricing arrangement
- the duration of the contract
- the preparation of the tender documents.

❑ Sourcing and supplier appraisal

In the list of value for money factors in chapter 1, the 'status of the firms involved' was shown as the point at which value for money, in all respects, begins.

The risk of obtaining poor value for money from a 'poor' supplier is a fact of life that can be experienced in Government procurement just as much as in our everyday lives.

Government purchasers, like the most professional of those in the private sector, need to deal with the best suppliers. The best can be thought of as those with whom the Government purchasing organisation is prepared to commit itself contractually on behalf of the taxpayer. Identifying them requires *sourcing* and *supplier appraisal*.

The definitions of sourcing and supplier appraisal are:

Sourcing - the identification and (where necessary) development of possible sources of supply.

Supplier Appraisal - the systematic investigation of these identified sources.

When considering the procurement cycle, 'sourcing' and 'supplier appraisal' were seen as activities occurring early on in the purchasing process. However, wherever possible, these should be part of a continuous process, linked to an effective 'vendor rating' scheme, as they are one of the keys to the achievement of value for money. Time invested in developing a sound supplier base pays off when unforeseeable events conspire to undermine a strategically important contract.

Where a purchase is made according to procedures prescribed by the EC Procurement Directives, the required advertising means that the sourcing and supplier appraisal phases must effectively be undertaken as part of each tender process. The Directives and the procedures prescribed are discussed more fully at chapter 11.

Sources of supply and supplier information

Although some small purchasing organisations rely upon an adhoc approach to this aspect of purchasing, others have formal sourcing procedures to enable themselves to remain up-to-date with changes in their particular market. A good understanding of the market is vital if a buyer is to negotiate successfully with knowledgeable suppliers. The main sourcing methods that may be adopted are described below. It is often the case that too little time is allowed in purchasing organisations for many (or even any) of them to be used effectively. It should be emphasised, though, that these methods only identify potential sources of supply. With the exception of discussions with other purchasers, they make little contribution to knowledge of the quality and effectiveness of the potential suppliers.

Trade journals – Specialised trade journals are available for most industries and can be an invaluable source of information about new suppliers and their products.

Trade directories – There are several of these available in the United Kingdom, such as Kelly's and Kompass. They contain information on the names and addresses of companies and the places of manufacture, stockists and service providers. The directories are often indexed by commodity and manufacturer.

Supplier catalogues – These are often used as a source of supplier information, both of products and price estimates. As explained in chapter 3, (the legal aspects of purchasing), catalogues frequently contain the supplier's terms and conditions of contract. These are obviously compiled to achieve the most favourable contractual arrangements for the company. However, they are not in themselves an offer to sell on those conditions at the price printed. The catalogue invites buyers to make an offer to purchase.

Visits from suppliers' representatives – All buyers receive visits from representatives of potential suppliers. It is possible for both parties to gain some knowledge and benefit from these meetings – the seller about the organisation and the products and services bought, the buyer about the company's organisation and the products and services generally sold. However, these meetings can be very time consuming and, although they may have a place in the sourcing process, it may be felt that the scarce time available for this activity could often be more productively employed. It should be recognised, though, that to deny a supplier the opportunity to make a sales presentation is to risk the loss of a new source of supply as well as the information that may have been gained during the interview.

Trade exhibitions – A trade exhibition can be a good provider of sourcing information. A visit to a relevant exhibition can give the purchaser access to a wealth of information upon current and potential suppliers, all under one roof and all in a day. However, to be effective, the approach needs to be systematic not just aimless wandering.

Discussions with other purchasers – Increasingly, Government purchasers are making use of the supplier information available in other departments, although, on a personal level, not all individuals are fully prepared to disclose their sources of supply. The sharing of relevant experiences when Government purchasers meet, on a course or seminar, can be a useful supplement to other, more formal, sourcing activities.

Advertising by the buying department – Apart from the methods outlined above, the sourcing activity for purchases made under the EC Procurement Directives is conducted by way of the Notice published in the Official Journal of the European Communities (OJEC). The Notice advertising the requirement to potential suppliers may bring to light many sources of supply, perhaps, on occasions, too many!

Supplier appraisal

Once potential sources of supply have been identified, the next step in seeking value for money, and value for money improvements, is systematic investigation of the sources to ensure that they have the potential to be satisfactory supply partners to a Government contract. The following approach, goes systematically through two stages of supplier appraisal:

- financial aspects
- commercial and technical aspects.

The approach does, of course, have to be tailored to meet the particular needs of the purchasing organisation. For example, the administratively costly supplier appraisal process may be simplified for straightforward, low value, low risk purchases. It is just possible, in these cases, that the sourcing information already available will be adequate alone, but great care needs to be exercised in contracting with a supplier without the knowledge gained by a supplier appraisal exercise.

The normal approach to obtaining the information required in a supplier appraisal is for the purchasing policy side of the government to start by drawing up a supplier questionnaire. This is normally completed by the supplier but that step may be followed by a supplier visit where the complexity and value of the requirement warrants such action. An example of a typical questionnaire in use is shown in Figure 4.2.

❏ Financial appraisal

It is unlikely, though not impossible, that a supplier with financial difficulties will be able to provide value for money. Continuity of supply and reliability of the product or service are just two value for money factors that may be jeopardised by contracting with a financially unstable supplier. It is essential to establish that the supplier has a high probability of being in existence not only for the duration of the contract but also some years after when post-contract issues may still need to be pursued.

General, financial and technical information required

1 Name of business to be registered, head office address, telephone, telex and fax numbers.

2 VAT number and/or tax certificate.

3 Name, address, telephone and telex number of major factories or branch offices.

4 If incorporated, details of all associated companies, subsidiaries, parent or holding companies, including full name, address and country in which registered.

5 Date of formation of the business or of incorporation, and brief history.

6 Details of business:

   (i)   If incorporated, state the full names of all directors, company secretary and other principal office holders, together with their position, private address, date and place of birth, and details of other directorships held. Similar information should be provided for individuals holding more than one-fifth of the paid-up shares, preference shares, or loan capital.

   (ii) If sole traders or partnership, state full name, position, private address, date and place of birth, and other directorships held, of all persons financially interested in the business.

7 Type of work for which you wish to be invited to tender, and geographic area (if appropriate).

8 Range of contract value normally undertaken.

9 General description of business.

10 Facilities, (manufacturing capacity, maintenance facilities).

11 Total area of works.

12 Total manufacturing area.

13 Number employed/principal trades/number skilled or unskilled.

14 Previous experience (please provide two full names and addresses of Government departments, local authorities, and key customers in private sector for whom work has been done, together with any references).

Figure 4.2 Supplier questionnaire (continued overleaf)

General, financial and technical information required

15 Details of documented procedures for control of quality.

16 Senior officials

    i) Head of organisation/works director

    ii) Executive responsible for design

    iii) Executive responsible for quality

    iv) Quality manager

17 Details of management structure (including QA organisation).

18 Of what Trade Association, if any, is the business a member?

19 Copies of audited accounts of the last two years and those of the group, if appropriate, should be provided. Parterships, sole traders and businesses formed within the last two years should provide management accounts if audited accounts are not available. If incorporated, please provide a copy of the latest annual return, details of any changes in the Register of Directors and Register of Charges made in the last twelve months.

20 Name and address of bankers.

21 Signature and date

I confirm that the information provided herein is to the best of my knowledge complete and accurate.

Signature   Date

Name and position held (eg Managing Director, Senior Partner, or Sole Trader)

Figure 4.2 (continued) Supplier questionnaire

To enable financial stability issues to be considered professionally by the purchasing organisation, qualified accountants are employed in some of the larger Government departments to analyse company balance sheets and profit and loss accounts. Other departments make use of specialist companies to examine and report on the financial status of potential suppliers. While Government purchasing staff are not expected to be financial analysts, they do need to be able to interpret financial reports, and to make use of key business ratios. In particular, the use of liquidity, profitability and efficiency ratios may give vital clues to a supplier's viability. In this chapter the following important ratios will be examined:

- return on capital employed
- current ratio
- quick ratio (or acid test)

- debtors turnover
- creditors turnover.

Return on capital employed

The profit motive is one of the driving forces of most commercial businesses, an incentive to greater efficiency and effectiveness. Better organisation, more effective methods or working, reduced unit costs and greater turnover all help to improve the level of profit. A common measure of a company's profitability is the return on capital employed. This ratio is frequently used both by the company and users of the company as an assessment of its performance and efficiency.

The figure of capital employed, can be derived from the company's Balance Sheet, by two main methods:

- the first concentrates on the sources of funds,

  Issued Share Capital + Reserves + Long Term Loans

- the second concentrates on the type of assets,

  Fixed Assets + (Current Assets - Current Liabilities)

Both methods produce the same figure. The capital employed, from a simplified version of a company's balance sheet, might appear as in Figure 4.3.

Both approaches take into account the total capital employed in the business and must be related to a measure of profit that does not separately distinguish between the return on shareholders' funds and the return on loan capital. That measure of profit is the *operating profit*, the amount of profit before the return on the loan capital (interest) is deducted.

By using the figure for operating profit (from the profit and loss account) as a measure of the company's return, and the capital employed (from the balance sheet) as a measure of the sum invested in the company, the following 'formula' is obtained:

% Return on Capital Employed

=

$$\frac{\text{Operating Profit}}{\text{Share Capital} + \text{Reserves} + \text{Loan Capital}} \times 100$$

	Year 2	Year 1
	£m	£m
METHOD 1		
Issued Share Capital eg 500,000 ordinary shares	300	300
Reserves eg share premium, P & L account, general reserve	37	31
Long Term Loans eg 10% debentures	100	–
	437	**331**
METHOD 2		
Fixed Assets eg land, buildings, plant and machinery, etc	305	202
Current Assets eg stock, work in progress, cash at bank and in hand, debtors, etc	356	331
	661	533
Less		
Current Liabilities eg creditors, bank loans, taxation, etc	**224**	**202**
	437	331

Figure 4.3 Capital employed

For example, taking the numbers from Figure 4.3, if the operating profit in Year 2 were £34 million, and in Year 1 were £32 million, then the return on capital employed for these years would be:

Year 2

$$\frac{34}{437} \times 100 = 7.8\%$$

Year 1

$$\frac{32}{331} \times 100 = 9.7\%$$

If the interpretation of profit and capital employed is consistent year by year, and if the profits are calculated and the assets valued on the same basis year by year, then the trend indicated by the ratios should be meaningful. It is also possible to compare alternative suppliers, but the notes to the accounts need to be examined closely to ensure that differences in accounting policies from company to company are not significant.

Current ratio

Liquidity ratios reflect the ability of the company to pay amounts owing as they fall due for payment. A company may be profitable in terms of return on capital employed, but if it does not have sufficient liquid assets to meet its current liabilities, those liabilities which are due for payment in the near future, it may be in a dangerous trading position.

The current ratio is sometimes known as the working capital ratio and is defined as:

$$\frac{\text{current assets}}{\text{current liabilities}}$$

Working capital (or net current assets) is the excess of current assets over current liabilities. In the normal course of business transactions, a company's non cash current assets, work in progress, stock and debtors, are eventually converted into cash. Work in progress is completed and becomes stock, stock is sold and becomes debtors, the debtors pay and the debt becomes 'cash'. Current assets may therefore be treated as cash and nearly cash, although just how near to cash those assets are depends on the nature of the stock and of the debtors.

The current ratio is therefore a simple measure of the company's ability to pay its short-term liabilities. If the current assets are greater than the current liabilities, the company should have no difficulty in paying its accounts as they become due.

In the simplified balance sheet in Figure 4.3, the current ratio for each year would be given by:

Year 2

$$\frac{356}{224} = 1.59$$

Year 1

$$\frac{331}{202} = 1.64$$

Therefore in Year 2, for every £1.00 of current liabilities, the company had £1.59 of current assets available. Similarly, in Year 1 the company had £1.64 of current assets available for £1.00 of current liabilities. It is sometimes said that this ratio should be near 2:1 for a company to be financially viable, although many reputable firms continue to exist with a much lower ratio. It is the trend from year to year which is important, together with the nature of the current assets. For example, there may be concern if current assets consist of large amounts of slow moving stock but only low levels of debtors and cash.

Quick ratio (or acid test)

Like the current ratio, the quick ratio is a liquidity ratio which aims to assess the ability of the company to pay its short-term liabilities. However, it is a tougher test of liquidity than the current ratio as it excludes one important element of current assets, namely stock. This is because, in some businesses, it might be unwise to include stock as a means of paying debts as it may take a long time to convert the stock into cash. It may be appropriate to include it in the case of shops selling perishable goods, but not in many others.

The quick ratio is defined as:

$$\frac{\text{Current assets LESS stock}}{\text{Current liabilities}}$$

It is sometimes said that the ratio should be around 1:1, but, as mentioned earlier, it is the trend that is important, coupled with some knowledge of the circumstances of how the company buys and sells to conduct its business.

If the values of stock for Year 1 and Year 2 were £50 million and £70 million respectively in the simplified balance sheet in Figure 4.3, the quick ratio would be:

Year 2	Year 1
$\dfrac{286}{224} = 1.28$	$\dfrac{281}{202} = 1.39$

So, in Year 2, for every £1.00 of current liability, the company had £1.28 available. Similarly, in Year 1, for every £1.00 of current liability, the company had £1.39 available.

However, this ratio assumes that the current asset, debtors, may be quickly converted into cash. This may not always be so. Long periods of credit may be the norm in the industry, or perhaps the debtors concerned are experiencing business difficulties. An indication of this is provided by the first efficiency ratio, the debtors/turnover ratio.

Debtors/turnover ratio

There are many efficiency ratios which, taken together, give an indication of how a company is being managed. They make use of a particular current asset or current liability from the balance sheet, expressed as a ratio of a related profit and loss account figure.

The first efficiency ratio to be considered is the average collection period for debtors, the debtors/turnover or debtors/sales ratio. This ratio reveals the time in which the company's average debt is settled. It is therefore an indication of the liquidity of this form of asset. This ratio is expressed in terms of a number of days:

$$\frac{\text{Trade debtors}}{\text{Sales}} \times 365$$

In effect, it shows how many days' worth of sales are represented by the level of debtors. One obvious proviso in connection with this ratio is that the sales figure must be for credit and not cash sales. As with the other ratios, an examination of the trend over a period and some comparison with the industry standard would prove most meaningful. For example, if the debtors started to take longer to pay, a reducing rate of cash flow into the company would result. This might stem from either slack credit control or an increase of bad debts.

Creditors/purchases ratio (payment period)

The second efficiency ratio to be considered here is the payment period or average period of credit taken by the company from its creditors. It is given by the following:

$$\frac{\text{Total creditors}}{\text{Total credit purchases}} \times 365 \text{ days}$$

An increase in this period might be an indication of cash flow problems causing the company to delay payment of its creditors. Alternatively it may indicate a change in company policy to seek the longest possible period of credit.

Government procurement organisations normally aim to pay their contractors within 30 days of receipt of a correctly completed invoice, often well within 30 days. They also try to ensure, by way of a contract condition, that their good practice of prompt payment is extended by the main contractor to its sub- contractors and so on throughout the private sector. This is an example of Government, through its substantial procurement activity, seeking positively to influence the behaviour of industry. The purpose is to alleviate the real hardship caused to smaller companies by the practice of paying late. The use of this ratio can highlight those businesses with a poor track record in this respect. However, this ratio is difficult to calculate because credit purchases are not always available from published accounts. In practice, the cost of sales figure is commonly used as a substitute, giving the ratio:

$$\frac{\text{Total creditors}}{\text{Cost of sales}} \times 365 \text{ days}$$

Use of ratio analysis

Trends in the ratios described above can be useful for a general assessment of a company's efficiency and financial stability. However, it is important to think carefully about the figures and the factors influencing them before any firm conclusions are reached. For example, it is important to look at the basis on which assets have been valued and the economic conditions within which the company has been operating. The accounting issues likely to arise are explained in another text in the present series (Archibald 1994).

Commercial and technical appraisal

Even though a supplier may be financially sound, a commercial and technical appraisal is required to ensure that the company has the means, in the form of buildings, equipment and personnel, to meet the requirements of a potential contract. In addition, evidence of a sound track record is required to reduce the level of risk that exists when any contract is made. The commercial and technical appraisal will require consideration of such details of the company as, for example:

- the quality management systems or other technical standards of competence
- the production capacity and capability to carry out the work using the appropriate tooling, plant and equipment
- the professional qualifications of the supplier's key personnel
- the details of principal deliveries and services provided over the previous three years; references or other documentary evidence should be sought
- the technical support which the supplier can call upon.

Supplier visits

Where necessary, for complex, critical and high value purchases, appraisal visits of potential suppliers will be required. These may be conducted by members of the procurement team and often include finance and quality assurance representatives to assess the financial, commercial and technical factors outlined above. The visit should include a tour of the company's facilities so that the atmosphere of the organisation can be felt, observations made and specific questions asked. It is vital that the visit is carefully planned, with questions prepared and 'things to look out for' thought through in advance. A typical visit might include coverage of such aspects as:

- adequacy of manufacturing/distribution facilities
- management's technical know-how and managerial capabilities
- R & D capability (if appropriate)
- effectiveness of production control
- existence and availability of quality manual
- technical/managerial competence
- morale of personnel, working conditions, and their enthusiasm
- approach to training
- staff turnover
- level of supervision and worker/supervisor relationships
- state of order book and quantity of outstanding orders

- age and state of plant and equipment, rate of output
- state of cleanliness/orderliness
- levels of raw materials, finished goods, work in progress.

Such visits to tend to bring to light major differences in standards demonstrating the need for this aspect of the appraisal process if overall value for money is to be achieved.

Sourcing/supplier appraisal and the tendering process

The importance of this phase in the procurement cycle cannot be overstressed and yet it is an area of procurement in Government which generally seems to deserve more resources. The pay-back is a reduced risk of purchasing difficulties once a contract has been awarded, when problems become far more costly to resolve.

As stated earlier in this chapter, sourcing and supplier appraisal should ideally be an on-going activity, part of a continuous supplier-base improvement process. In practice, this often does not happen. A reactive approach is more commonly encountered in departments. This could be for a number of reasons:

- resources are frequently scarce
- the value of this phase of procurement is underrated
- EC Procurement Directives focus this activity on particular purchase requirements (see chapter 11).

It has already been suggested that professional purchasers, in central Government or the private sector, generally want to deal with only good suppliers. The description of a good supplier, written by Professor Wilbur B England of Harvard University, is frequently encountered in purchasing texts. It goes as follows:

> A good supplier is one who is at all times honest and fair in his dealing with the customers, his own employees, and himself; who has adequate plant facilities and know-how so as to be able to provide materials which meet the purchaser's specifications, in the quantities required, and at the time promised; whose financial position is sound; whose prices are reasonable both to the buyer and to himself; whose management policies are progressive; who is alert to the need for continued improvement in both his products and his manufacturing processes; and who realises that, in the last analysis, his own interests are best served when he best serves his customers.

Government purchasing organisations are unlikely to be fortunate enough just to stumble across a supplier like that described above. Such suppliers need to be carefully sought out, not only to ensure the successful completion of an individual contract or series of contracts but also, on the macro-economic scale of Government procurement, to ensure that the positive effects of competition and

❏ The Invitation to Tender

In straightforward cases, the invitation to tender will normally contain at least:

- the instructions to tenderers
- the specification
- the terms and conditions that will apply to any resulting contract
- a price schedule.

For more complex requirements, each tenderer may be asked to provide, for example:

- a detailed description of how the tenderer proposes to meet the performance requirements of each task and the contract as a whole
- a quality plan covering the objectives of the specification
- details of proposed sub-contractors
- a detailed programme for meeting the requirement during the transitional stage.

In order that the competition is fair to all concerned, each tenderer must be asked to submit their offer on the same basis, meaning that all invitations to tender for a particular requirement must be identical. This also applies to the time allowed for the tender period, any extension granted, additional information that may be provided during the tender period, and so on.

❏ Tender opening boards

In view of the large sums involved in Government purchasing and the need to be fully accountable at each stage of the tendering process, great care should be taken to ensure that completed tenders are handled with due regard for equity and propriety. Quite clearly a system is required to ensure that:

- premature disclosure of prices and other information is not possible
- complete transparency can be demonstrated.

professional purchasing have an impact on the economies of the UK and European Union as a whole.

To meet this requirement, tenders are stored until the due date for opening in a secure place–quite frequently, in practice, in a double-locked tender box requiring two different keys to open. It is then normally the task of a formally constituted tender board, comprising a purchasing branch member, an independent member and a secretary, to open the tender box and the tender documents on the due date. At this stage, some departments emboss the tender documents to prevent additional documents being added at a later date in an attempt to influence the contract award decision. The documents will at least be initialled and stamped by the board and, in addition, alterations to typed figures highlighted and recorded. From this point, any subsequent alterations attempted by any of those handling the tender documents at a later date would be obvious. Furthermore, it can be clearly demonstrated, should a challenge arise, that there was no opportunity for such irregularities to occur.

❏ Managing the contract

Even though the private sector supplier and the Government department are contractually bound as a result of the competitive tendering process, this is no guarantee that the contract will be discharged to the buyer's satisfaction. Effective sourcing, supplier appraisal and contract award procedures will minimise the risk of dealing with an unsuitable supplier, but effective contract management will ensure that:

- the contractor's performance is maintained
- problems and changes required are anticipated
- the contract terms and conditions are met
- documented evidence of good performance is recorded to demonstrate the achievement of value for money
- documented evidence of bad performance is recorded to permit early recourse to the department's rights under the default provisions.

❏ Vendor rating

The systematic assessment of suppliers *before* a contract is awarded is known as *supplier appraisal*; objective assessment in numerical terms *after* a contract has been completed is known as *vendor rating*. It is a process of objective scoring to help suppliers improve their performance and to contribute to future decisions about their suitability.

Each particular contract, however straightforward or complex, will have its successes and failures during the course of its life. Much can be learnt from each success and even more can be taught by each failure if a systematic approach to rating the performance of the contractor is practised. Vendor rating frequently covers, among others, such aspects of the supplier's performance as:

- quality
- delivery
- price
- administrative effectiveness.

If it is intended to rate suppliers against these factors, they would first be weighted to reflect their importance to the purchasing organisation. For example, in Figure 4.4 quality and price have equal importance, delivery is third and administration fourth.

	Factor	Maximum Points
A	Quality	35
B	Delivery	20
C	Price	35
D	Administrative effectiveness	10
	Total	100

Figure 4.4 Vendor rating, example of factor weighting

A perfect supplier could achieve a maximum of 100 points if they performed the contract with no quality or delivery failures, they were the most price competitive and answered letters and submitted invoices correctly and promptly. However, a less able supplier may have had:

- a quality failure rate of 5 per cent
- made 8 per cent of deliveries over one week late
- a price that was £10.00 each more than the lowest price
- five administrative failures at 6 per cent for each failure.

Each element of contract performance data can be converted into an appropriate score and applied to the weighted performance factor as shown in Figure 4.5. The price performance is a measure of the lowest price offered divided by the actual price paid.

		Maximum points	Actual performance	Performance evaluation	
A	*Quality*	35	5% rejects	$35 \times 95\% =$	33.25
B	*Delivery*	20	8% late	$20 \times 92\% =$	18.40
C	*Price*	35	£100	$35 \times \dfrac{£90}{£100} =$	31.50
D	*Administrative effectiveness*	10	5 failures	$10 \times 70\% =$	7.00
	Max Total	**100**	**Overall evaluation**	$=$	**90.15**

Figure 4.5 Vendor rating factors and weighting

Although Figure 4.5 illustrates only a simple example, the value of effective vendor rating in achieving progressive supplier improvement cannot be overstated. Vendor rating is quite a common practice in the private sector and is employed mainly in respect of a company's major suppliers so that each small improvement achieved brings correspondingly greater benefits. More and more purchasing organisations in Government recognise that the purchasing cycle is incomplete without an element of vendor rating and subsequent action.

Reference

Archibald, V (1994) *Accruals Accounting in the Public Sector* Harlow Longman.

England, W B *(1967) Procurement Principles and Cases* Homewood, Ill. Richard D. Irwin.

Official Journal of the European Communities (OJEC) Luxembourg, Office for official publications of the European Community.

Chapter 5

Types of contract used in Government purchasing –

the approach to pricing

Depending on the nature of the goods or services purchased by a Government procurement organisation, it may be possible for the purchaser to remain ignorant of the contractor's costs of production and yet still be able to achieve value for money for the taxpayer. For example, in a fully competitive environment, the workings of the market should ensure that the prices charged for any given quality of product or level of service do not produce excessive profit for the supplier.

However, there are circumstances where a deeper understanding of how a contractor incurs and recovers costs may offer possibilities for exploiting potential value for money improvements. This understanding should form part of the basic knowledge of a professional purchaser, and certainly does so in many parts of the central Government purchasing organisation.

Contractor's costs

On occasions, when a price breakdown is requested from a supplier, costs can be shown under a series of headings which, taken together with the profit element, add up to the price. A typical price breakdown for a manufactured product is shown in Figure 5.1. Types of cost shown in Figure 5.1 will now be considered individually.

❏ Direct costs

Direct costs are those costs which are directly attributable, in full, to the product concerned. The direct costs in the breakdown are the direct labour costs (machine shop and assembly shop), the raw materials, the subcontract costs and the cost of bought-in finished parts. All of these direct costs can be physically identified (and measured) against a specific product.

	£
Raw materials	124.50
Machine shop labour costs	1072.50
(165 hours @ £6.50 per hour)	
Machine shop overheads @ 280%	3003.00
Assembly shop labour costs	81.90
(14 hours @ £5.85 per hour)	
Assembly shop overheads @ 170%	139.23
Subcontracts	93.00
Bought-in finished parts	27.86
TOTAL COSTS	4541.99
Profit @ 7.8%	354.28
PRICE QUOTED	4896.27

Figure 5.1 Example of typical price breakdown for manufactured product

If the company providing the breakdown were in the executive furniture business, for example, the raw materials might comprise tubular steel, purchased to be formed into the frame of a chair, and steel wire, to be formed into springs. A definite amount of tubular steel and steel wire is required and can be identified for the manufacture of the executive chair. The costs in respect of the bought-in finished parts may relate to a number of castors and a single gas-lift device, components which are required but not made in-house. In addition, sub-contract costs may be incurred, perhaps for the chromium plating of the tubular steel frame once it has been formed, because there is no plating facility in the furniture factory.

Direct labour costs

Direct labour costs are those labour costs which can be specifically identified with a particular product. In the example above, there are two forms of direct labour cost:

- machine shop – the wages of employees who make the parts
- assembly shop – the wages of employees who assemble the parts, both those made in-house and those purchased outside.

The appearance of a price-breakdown will vary widely, depending upon the goods or services purchased, but it will have much in common with that shown in Figure 5.1. For example, there may not always be two types of labour; there may be more or fewer, but the principles will be the same.

❑ Indirect costs

The costs considered so far are those which can be traced in full to a particular product. However, many costs incurred by a company cannot be specifically identified with a particular product. These are known as *indirect costs* and commonly referred to as a contractor's *overheads*.

Overheads and method of recovery

Some possible examples of indirect costs or overheads incurred by a contractor are as follows:

- business rates
- rent
- gas
- electricity
- depreciation
- post
- telephones
- indirect labour costs.

Examples of indirect labour costs could be:

- security
- personnel
- staff restaurant personnel
- machine shop supervisor
- assembly shop supervisor
- maintenance personnel
- quality engineer
- management and administration personnel.

All of these costs are incurred for the benefit of groups of products or all products; none can be identified with any one specific product. However, at the end of the day, they all need to be recovered within the price of goods sold by the company if it is to remain in business. Overhead recovery needs to be achieved in a way such that each product manufactured or service provided by the company attracts a fair proportion of these indirect costs, so as not to distort the price competitiveness of the product or service in the market place. Consider now how this often works in practice.

Percentage overhead rates

In the price breakdown seen at Figure 5.1, some percentage overhead rates were used. These are very common but not always understood. To illustrate their use, imagine wanting to invest money in a new, prestige garage workshop. Before leaping into the project, it would be wise to carry out some market research, in an attempt to quantify the potential demand for the service. Assuming that the research identified sufficient demand, at the right end of the market, the next step is to look for premises in which to house the garage workshop facility. They would need to be of an appropriate size to meet current anticipated demand, perhaps with room for expansion. Then we could recruit our labour force to meet our anticipated needs. At this stage, assume that we have identified the following factors that will affect our approach to pricing any work to be carried out in the garage:

Estimated number of cars to be serviced and/or repaired per annum	2000
Direct labour costs Five garage mechanics @ £15,000 per annum (£7.50 an hour for a 40 hour week for 50 weeks)	£ 75,000.00
Indirect costs/overheads business rates, heating, lighting, insurance, depreciation, etc	£150,000.00

From this information, it is possible to decide how to charge our customers in order to recover the direct and indirect costs we expect to incur over the year. Ignore profit for the time being, and assume that any parts and materials will be charged at cost. The question is, what method should be used to recover the overhead costs? Before looking at a sensible approach, it may be useful, for comparison purposes, to consider a recovery method that could well lead to bankruptcy.

From the market research, it was anticipated that the workload would be 2000 cars per annum, against which it would be necessary to recover overhead costs of £150,000.00. Why not then charge each customer the direct labour costs booked to the particular job, at £7.50 an hour, plus parts and materials, and a further £75.00 (ie £150,000.00 shared between 2000 customers) to contribute to the total overhead bill? In this way, the direct costs of parts and labour will have been met and, at the end of the year, 2000 customers will have met the overhead cost of £150,000.00 per annum.

The flaw in this simple approach is probably quite obvious. Some of the 2000 customers may only want a new tyre for their car or a new fuse or a change of oil. It is unlikely that they will be willing to pay £75.00 on top of parts and labour costs. Conversely, the prices will look very attractive to car owners whose engine or gearbox needs a major repair, and there could be a flood of such customers. The workload will consist of clients wanting time-consuming work while the same people will go to competitors for the minor work. The effect of this will be that, because of the nature of the workload, the throughput may only be, say, 1200 cars with a £75.00 contribution to overheads per car, the operation will only recover enough to pay £90,000.0 of the £150,000.00 overhead bill. Bankruptcy is not far away!

What is really needed is a recovery method which apportions the overhead costs in a more equitable way, with the more complicated and time-consuming jobs generally attracting a higher proportion of the total overhead bill. So, in the example of the garage, it would be better to relate overheads to time spent on a particular job. The more complex, and time-consuming the work, the greater the amount of overheads it should attract. The direct labour costs can be used as the measure of complexity as they are directly related to time. This approach allows the garage to remain competitive across a range of work.

Where indirect costs are recovered as a proportion of the direct labour costs, the overhead rate 'formula' is given by the following:

$$\frac{\text{Indirect costs}}{\text{Direct labour costs}} \times 100 = \text{percentage overhead rate to be applied to the direct labour costs}$$

This is not the only method of overhead recovery used, but it is very common in many types of industry. In the garage example, the overhead rate for work carried out in the coming year can be calculated as follows:

$$\frac{\text{Indirect costs (estimated for the coming year)}}{\text{Direct labour costs (estimated for the coming year)}} \times 100$$

giving:

$$\frac{£150,000}{£75,000} \times 100 = 200\%$$

An overhead rate of 200% applied to direct labour costs will achieve a £2.00 contribution towards the indirect costs for every £1 of direct labour cost incurred. If five mechanics are kept working for the full year, with no slack time and no overtime, in theory the sum of all the invoices raised might look like this:

Direct labour costs		
10,000 hours @ £7.50 per hour	=	£ 75,000.00
(ie 5 mechanics @ 40 hours per week for 50 weeks)		
Indirect costs		
Overhead rate @ 200%	=	£150,000.00
(applied to direct labour costs ie £75,000)		
Parts and materials at cost	=	£ 55,000.00
Total cost	=	£280,000.00
Profit on costs at, say, 15%	=	£ 42,000.00
Grand total of all invoices issued	=	£322,000.00

In reality, of course, this amount of detail would not be revealed on each invoice. (To provide such information without being asked for it could prompt some of the customers to challenge the detail and the garage would not wish to encourage negotiation.) So instead the invoices will show an 'all-up' rate or 'inclusive rate' *for each hour of direct labour expended*. This inclusive rate will cover the wages element, the overheads and the profit element, giving:

	£
1 hour @ £7.50 per hour	7.50
Overheads @ 200%	15.00
Total cost per hour	22.00
Profit @ 15%	3.30
Inclusive 'cost' per hour	25.30

In other words, a 'labour' rate of £25.30 an hour will be quoted. The price shown in the break-down at Figure 5.1 was not calculated on the basis of an 'all-up' rate but showed each element separately.

Such a price breakdown is often required by a purchasing organisation, to satisfy itself about the elements of the price. In Figure 5.1, two separate overhead rates were used, implying that the company concerned had two *cost centres*. This simply means that the indirect costs associated with the machine shop and the assembly shop are treated separately and recovered against the machine shop direct labour costs and the assembly shop direct labour costs respectively. Cost centres can be a person, a machine or part of a factory. Once they are set up, costs incurred can be charged to cost centres using an appropriate cost coding system, providing the company with product or service cost information.

Types of contract pricing in central Government procurement

In thinking about pricing it may be right to start by considering a supplier's costs of manufacturing a product or providing a service. However, one of the responsibilities of any purchasing organisation is to obtain the products or services required at the '*right price*'. Purchasing professionals generally take the right price to mean a 'price which is fair and reasonable to both parties'. Many variables will influence a supplier's view of what constitutes a 'fair and reasonable price' for example:

- their position in the market
- the strength of the competition
- their marketing skills
- their costs.

In a dynamic commercial environment, the right price for one supplier, at a particular point in time, is unlikely to be the same price as that of another supplier.

In Government, professional purchasers aim to obtain goods and services at the right price by making use of competitive tendering wherever practicable and practical, it being a principle of central Government procurement that competitive tendering should be adopted unless there are convincing reasons to the contrary. However, competitive tendering is only one way of arriving at a price and some others will be considered later in this chapter.

❑ Firm price contracts

Just as there are many ways to *arrive* at a contract price, there are also many *types* of price. It is a further principle of Government contracting that *firm price* contracts should be used wherever possible. Firm prices are those prices not subject to any provision for variation. In Government, a price which *is* subject to a variation of price (VOP) condition is known as a *fixed price*, and these will be considered later in this chapter.

Firm price contracts are the most desirable type of contract for a purchaser because they give the supplier the strongest incentive for economy and performance. For most Government organisations, firm price contracts are established from competitive tendering. However, because of the nature of their purchases, some bodies arrive at firm prices by cost analysis and negotiation.

Firm price contracts, especially those awarded by competition, have many advantages. They require a minimum of administration, (no auditing of costs,) and, as stated above, they give the contractor the maximum incentive to produce efficiently. In meeting the contract requirement, each pound by which the contractor 'beats' the price, is a pound 'in their pocket.' The contractor is incentivised to control costs and spend as little as necessary to meet the contract requirement. Given the scale of Government expenditure, the encouragement of more efficient suppliers can lead to a positive effect on the economy of the UK as a whole, (and indeed for all of Europe where contracts are awarded under EC Procurement Directives). Government will also benefit directly from the higher levels of efficiency when it comes to award future contracts.

Another advantage of firm price contracts is that all the <u>financial</u> risks are borne by the contractor. No change in the price is allowed for, and so 100% of any costs incurred *above* the price are met by the company.

With a firm price contract, therefore:

    (a) all the cost 'savings' below the price are kept by the contractor

    (b) all the costs incurred above the price are met by the contractor.

Later on this chapter introduces methods of pricing whereby cost savings and cost overruns are *shared* between the buyer and the seller.

So far it has been assumed that, with a firm price contract, the contractor still has a strong commitment to meet the contract requirement, whatever the cost outcome. However, the risk of product or service performance failure by the contractor is probably greater with this type of pricing arrangement than with any other, particularly if proper sourcing and supplier appraisal has not been carried out as part of the procurement process. In Figure 5.2, risks to the purchaser are considered for different types of pricing arrangement.

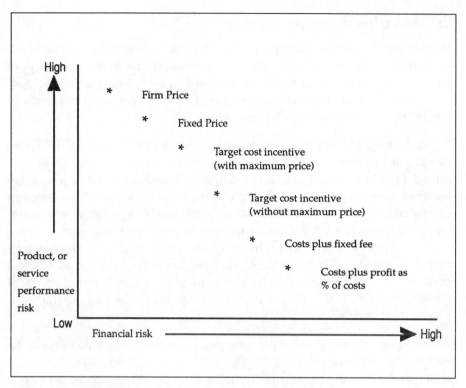

Figure 5.2 Risks of different pricing arrangements to a purchaser

Figure 5.2 shows the financial risk to Government with a firm price contract to be low. This is because the financial commitment made by Government is known from the moment that the firm price is agreed, (usually from the outset by competitive tender), and will not change. However, the figure also suggests that the risk of the contract requirement not being fully met is higher with this type of pricing arrangement than with others. With a firm price, the contractor keeps 100 per cent of every pound which they avoid spending under the contract, (though remaining bound to meet the terms of the contract.) If these cost savings are made by legitimate means, for example, increased efficiency and quicker delivery, then both parties to the contract would reap some benefit. However, it is not difficult to imagine that an unscrupulous supplier may care nothing for efficiency gains and be prepared to risk breaching the contract in some way so to make as large a profit as possible under the contract, taking the chance that no action will be taken against them. Insufficient attention to the supplier appraisal process in conjunction with firm price contracts can frequently lead to a poor contract outcome.

❑ Costs plus profit percentage

What about the pricing arrangements of the type at the opposite end of the graph at Figure 5.2? This type of pricing is called a 'costs plus profit as a percentage of costs' arrangement, and is usually abbreviated in everyday language to 'cost-plus.' It is not commonly used in Government procurement, but it still exists for specific reasons in one or two departments.

Figure 5.2 suggests this pricing arrangement as being of high financial risk and of low product or service performance risk to the Government. They are of high financial risk because the price is based upon the contractor's costs, reasonably incurred in carrying out the work or providing the service, plus a sum for profit calculated as a percentage of the costs. In other words, the greater the costs incurred by the contractor, the greater the level of profit achieved under the contract. Whereas the firm price contract 'rewards' a contractor for keeping their costs low, a cost-plus contract incentivises the contractor to spend as much as possible. There is a disincentive for the contractor to control their costs, and a disincentive to be more efficient, or to buy more wisely the raw materials and finished parts needed.

At the outset of a cost-plus contract, the purchaser has only a broad idea of the eventual financial commitment, despite all the safeguards which are frequently built into these types of contract to try to avoid cost overruns. These safeguards may include:

- weekly or monthly financial reports of expenditure and technical progress
- financial and technical progress meetings
- cost auditing on completion.

Such procedures make cost-plus contracts very costly to administer. In addition, it is only too easy, without firm discipline in the procurement team, to keep expanding the contract requirement (with perhaps a little encouragement from the contractor) so that the final version bears little resemblance to the original. Needless to say, the contractor is only too willing to accommodate these additions as the more they spend, the more profit they make! This last point is why these contracts may be viewed as of low product (or service) performance risk; the product or service, when eventually provided (if ever) should be of a very high standard. However this is not automatically so, as poor control in financial areas can spread to other areas within the contractor's organisation.

Figure 5.2 showed risks to the purchaser from different approaches to pricing. The equivalent diagram drawn from the contractor's point of view would be the mirror image of Figure 5.2.

In the case of the firm price arrangement, the performance risk remains at a high level, but the financial risk has moved from its low position for the purchaser to high for the contractor. This is because the contractor is at risk of making a loss if the contract costs exceed the firm price agreed. The more realistic the agreed price, the greater the risk of an unfavourable outcome for the contractor. However, there is also great potential to make very large profits if the agreed price is in any way generous or if significant cost savings can be achieved by the contractor.

For a cost plus profit arrangement, the performance risk remains at a low level, but the financial risk has moved from its high position, for the purchaser, to low for the contractor. This is because there is no risk of the contractor making a loss as the price is based on whatever (reasonable) costs are incurred with profit added as a percentage of those costs. The only thing which a cost plus profit arrangement lacks from the contractor's point of view is the potential for increasing profitability in those cases where costs can be kept low and the price undercut by significant margins.

The cost-plus profit contract is an example of a contract price based upon ascertained costs. Figure 5.2 shows three other examples of cost-based prices, namely,

- costs plus fixed fee
- target cost incentive, with maximum price
- target cost incentive, without maximum price.

These can only be used where the buying organisation has sufficient confidence in the contractor's cost-recording system and where the contract includes a condition giving the purchaser full rights to investigate the costs incurred if it is felt to be necessary.

It is often useful to compare different pricing methods in graphical form. Figure 5.3 shows the relationship of costs to the level of profit for a cost plus profit pricing arrangement.

It shows that the greater the costs, the larger the amount of profit. For example, if the costs incurred in meeting the contract requirement were £100K, and if the profit rate accepted by the purchaser were 10 per cent, the amount of profit would be £10K. If to meet the requirement the costs incurred by the contractor had been £200K, then the amount of profit would have been £20K. The graph clearly illustrates the point that the greater the costs, the greater the profit.

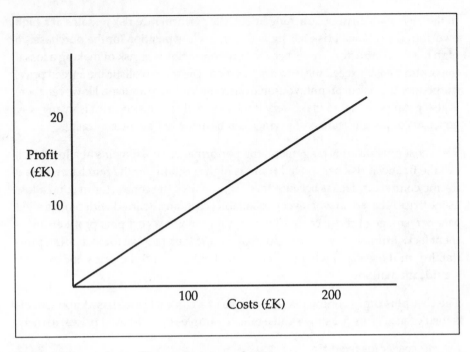

Figure 5.3 Costs plus profit as a percentage of costs

❏ Costs plus fixed fee

The first step towards making the cost plus profit approach to pricing mildly more of an incentive to the contractor to contain the company's costs is the 'costs plus fixed fee' price. This is illustrated in Figure 5.4 where the simple relationship between price and profit, (usually referred to here as the 'fee',) is shown.

Figure 5.4 shows, not surprisingly in view of the name, that whatever the contractor's out-turn cost in meeting the requirement, the amount paid by way of a fee (or profit) is constant. Consequently, there is a small incentive for the contractor to manage the costs. This is because, as Figure 5.4 shows, the rate of return on costs of £100K (10 per cent in this case) is *twice* the rate of return on costs of £200K (5 per cent). So with a price based upon costs plus a fixed fee, the amount of the fee (profit) remains constant, but the rate of return decreases as costs increase.

Although in normal circumstances there is a mild disincentive for the contractor to incur additional costs, there is a danger when using this type of pricing arrangement with a company whose order book is half empty. This is because the company might be only too willing to use your cost plus fixed fee contract as a means of recovering as many of their direct and indirect costs as possible, for as long as possible, until better times arrive. This company will not be concerned about making much profit but will be quite happy to recover its costs.

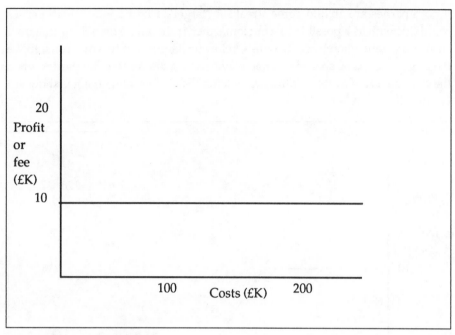

Figure 5.4 Costs plus fixed fee

❏ Target cost incentive arrangement

The next step towards giving the contractor more of an incentive to manage costs is the 'target cost incentive' approach. So far we have graphically considered cost plus profit and cost plus fixed fee pricing methods. The line in the first graph (Figure 5.3) slopes upwards, from left to right, indicating a proportionate increase in profit for each increase in cost, whereas in the second case (Figure 5.4) the line is horizontal, indicating a fixed reward for the contractor whatever the cost outturn.

A target cost incentive pricing arrangement would show a line sloping *downwards*, from left to right, so that the fee *reduces* as the costs *increase*. This approach should increase the contractor's incentive to manage the costs, because the *more* that is spent, the *lower* the profit. This arrangement might be used where, because of the nature of the work, there were many uncertainties about the requirement, making even a moderately accurate cost estimate difficult to compile. Imagine that a procurement organisation's possibly optimistic estimate of a contractor's costs for a project is about £80K, whereas the contractor's pessimistic cost estimate is £120K. If both parties are in a firm price environment the outcome with this scenario, even with the best negotiators, would probably be stalemate. However, a target cost incentive approach to pricing in these circumstances makes allowance for a range of possible cost outcomes while maintaining a reasonable incentive for contractor efficiency and effectiveness.

If both parties are able to agree a realistic 'target', a figure which both parties could live with as a possible cost outcome, then it should be feasible to construct an arrangement whereby cost savings, below the target, and cost overruns, above the target, would be shared in some way between the contracting parties when the costs are known after contract completion. Such an arrangement is shown in Figure 5.5.

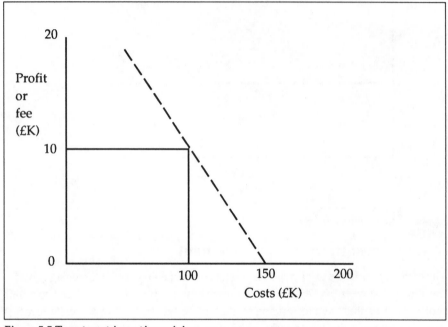

Figure 5.5 Target cost incentive pricing

Figure 5.5 includes some information which we have not seen before:

- a target cost
- a target fee
- a share ratio.

These are explained below.

Figure 5.5 shows that a target cost of £100K has been agreed between the buyer and seller and, if the acceptable profit rate is 10 per cent, the target fee is £10K. In other words, if the contractor's costs for meeting the contract requirement were £100K, they would be paid a fee of £10K, giving a price of £110K.

What would be the outcome if the contractor was able to *beat* the target cost? Imagine that the costs incurred in meeting the contract requirement were £80K, beating the target by £20K. How should this cost saving of £20K be shared between the purchaser and the contractor? In Figure 5.5, a typical share ratio of 80/20 is illustrated, indicating that any saving below the target would be shared in those proportions, the purchaser receiving 80 per cent of the saving and the contractor 20per cent. Therefore the price paid to the contractor would be arrived at as follows:

	£
Costs incurred	80,000.00
PLUS target fee	10,000.00
PLUS 20 % proportion of £20K cost saving	4,000.00
PRICE	94,000.00

The total fee or profit is then £14000. This can be seen graphically in Figure 5.6.

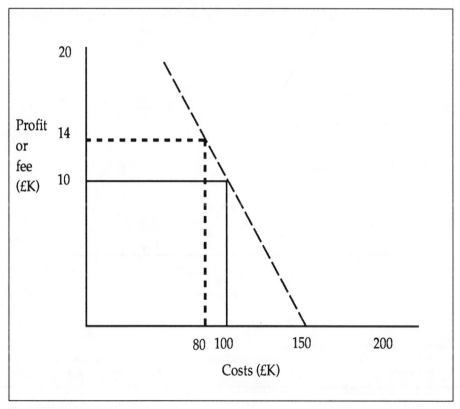

Figure 5.6 Beating the target cost

What price would be paid if the contractor *exceeded* the target cost by £20K? This would be calculated as follows:

	£
	£
Costs incurred	120,000.00
PLUS target fee	10,000.00
LESS 20% proportion of £20K cost overrun	- 4,000.00
PRICE	126,000.00

The total fee or profit would then be £6000. This can be seen graphically in Figure 5.7.

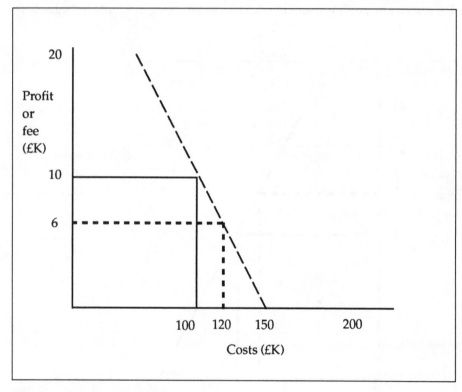

Figure 5.7 Exceeding the target cost

So, for every possible cost outcome, there is a price based upon the target cost, target fee and the sharing arrangement.

❑ Target cost incentive arrangement with maximum and minimum fee

It should be noted, with the example used above and an unlimited sharing arrangement, that, should the contractor's costs reach £150K, the fee received would be zero. It would be likely for a contractor to resist such an approach and instead look for a minimum fee, which would be paid whatever the cost outcome. In return for this minimum fee arrangement, the procurement organisation would probably want to see a limit set on the possible level of fee achieved. A target cost arrangement with a maximum and minimum fee is illustrated in Figure 5.8. The case illustrated assumes the same 80:20 sharing arrangement as in Figures 5.5, 5.6 and 5.7, but the maximum fee is set at £18K and the minimum at £2K.

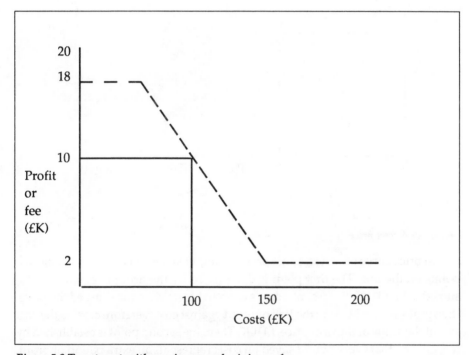

Figure 5.8 Target cost with maximum and minimum fee

❑ Firm price

So far graphs have been used only to illustrate cost-based prices. For comparison purposes, it would be useful to consider the picture of a firm price. When discussing firm prices earlier, it was said that a contractor meeting the requirement and spending *less* than the contract price in doing so, would *keep* 100 per cent of that 'saving'. Similarly, a contractor spending *more* than the contract price would have to *meet* 100 per cent of any costs incurred above the price. In 'share ratio' terms, this is a 0/100 arrangement. The purchaser would share *NONE* of the savings or overruns and the contractor would keep *ALL* of the savings or overruns. A graphical illustration of a firm price is shown in Figure 5.9.

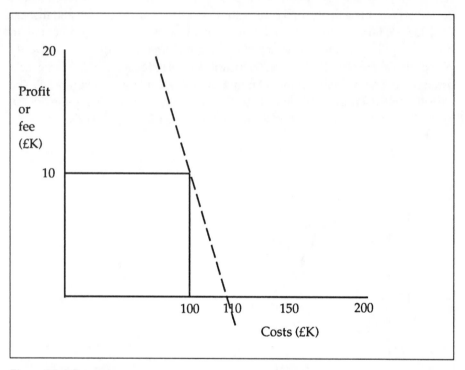

Figure 5.9 A firm price

A firm price curve of costs against profit is simply arrived at by determining two points on the line. The first point is determined by the firm price, which is assumed to be £110K. If the contractor's eventual costs were the same as the price, then profit would be zero; the line of profit against cost therefore crosses the cost axis at the value of the firm price, £110K. Then, the second point is established by recognising that every pound saved on costs represents an extra pound of profit, so that, for example, if costs are £100K, profit will be £10K.

Figure 5.9 shows that, for a firm price, the cost versus profit curve is very steep, and continues into to the 'negative profit' region. This illustrates the point made earlier in this chapter, that great opportunities exist for the contractor to make very large profits, or losses. Because of the relatively narrow range between large profits and significant losses, suppliers will naturally want to 'buffer' themselves from operating too near the 'real' price and so, given the opportunity, will quote high. This opportunity will be limited if the market is genuinely competitive.

❑ Target cost incentive with a maximum price

One of the drawbacks of the target cost arrangements considered so far is the relatively high financial risk which still exists for the procurement organisation. With each of the approaches considered, the ultimate financial commitment to the purchaser is unknown, because the final price is dependent, in some way, upon the contractor's costs. One way round this difficulty is to incorporate a maximum (firm) price into the target cost arrangement. The maximum possible financial commitment is then known, even though it would be hoped by both parties to the contract that the maximum price would remain a hypothetical one and would not be used for real. Consider Figure 5.10, which shows a target cost arrangement with a maximum price.

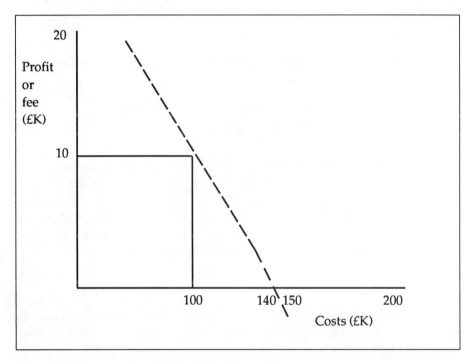

Figure 5.10 Target cost incentive with maximum price

In this diagram the target cost is again £100K, the target fee is £10K, and the share ratio is 80/20. The operation of the arrangement shown is very much the same as a target cost incentive *without* a maximium price, except that there is an upper limit to the price that will be paid; a maximum price. The maximum price in the example in Figure 5.10 is £142K. The slope of the dashed line changes at a cost of £140K. If costs are £140K, applying the 80/20 ratio to costs above £100K gives a fee of £2K and therefore a price of £142K. If costs rise above £140K, each extra £1K on costs reduces the fee by £1K. If costs turn out to be £150K the contractor will make a loss of £8K.

With a maximum price target cost incentive, the line takes two slopes. The first reflects the 80/20 share ratio, the second, with a share ratio of 0/100, reflects the effects of the maximum price, from a point where all additional costs are met by the contractor.

Pricing and contract duration

One of the strategic issues for consideration in purchasing is the contract duration. Should one opt for a longer duration contract, say three to five years, and take more of a 'partnership' approach to procurement, or should one aim to use the competitive market-place frequently to seek a better deal? Whatever the choice, it is important to understand the influences of a longer term contract on the price and to be aware of the pricing options which can be used to achieve overall value for money objectives.

Earlier in this chapter, we defined the terms 'firm price' and 'fixed price' as they are used in government procurement. By way of reminder:

- a firm price *is not* subject to any provision for variation
- a fixed price *is* subject to a price variation clause.

Government policy is that firm prices should be obtained for all contracts of under two years duration. This is because, as suggested in Figure 5.2, the level of financial risk to the department is less with a firm price than with a fixed price, except in those rare circumstances where it is known that the market price is falling, in which case a different contract strategy would be adopted. A fixed price contract, one with a price variation formula or, more loosely, one with an arrangement for an annual price review, reduces the financial risk to the contractor and increases it for the purchaser.

In compiling a firm price quotation for a product to be delivered or a service to be provided for a period of, say, three years, some of the factors which must be considered by a company are as follows:

- the cost estimate (at today's rates)
- the amount of competition
- its need for the work
- its position in the market place, and whether there is a desire to change it
- its view of future economic factors and their influence on wage rates, overheads, cost of raw materials, and so on.

Imagine a company quoting for the provision of a weekly service for a period of three years, which has calculated the price breakdown shown in Figure 5.11 at current rates. At what firm price should it tender?

	£
Raw materials	185.50
Labour	
80 hours @ 4.96 per hour	396.80
Overheads @ 182% of labour costs	
722.18	
Total costs	1304.48
Profit @ 8.2%	106.97
Price per week	1411.45

Figure 5.11 Illustrative price breakdown for provision of weekly service

Should the company tender at £1411.45 per week for the next three years? Should it quote a price which includes a wage increase of 3 per cent per annum and a materials increase of 2 per cent per annum, giving an average price of £1452.08 for the three years? Or, as it would dearly like this three year contract and because it knows the competition is fierce, should it quote a price of £1350.00 a week and strive to do the work more efficiently and effectively?

Alternatively does it wish to quote a firm price at all? If it can persuade the Government department to consider a fixed price, it will be much happier, particularly if it anticipates erratic increases in costs. If the workforce demand higher wages during the course of the contract, it will be better able to meet their claim if the price is automatically upwardly revised upwards; if the cost of raw materials increases significantly, it will similarly be able to recover those increased costs in the revised price.

The trouble is that if all parts of industry were to use only fixed prices, then inflation could soon increase dramatically as the incentive of firm prices was removed. Suppliers would be less concerned to keep costs down by being more efficient and effective in manufacturing the goods or providing the service. That is why Government policy on fixed prices is as it is. Fixed prices are considered more inflationary than firm prices, and they increase the financial risk and uncertainty to Government. Suppliers' preference for fixed prices as opposed to firm prices for contracts with a duration greater than two years is, at the time of writing, very weak. With inflationary pressures as they are now it is currently a relatively low risk to have to estimate now the cost of labour in two or three years time.

When the purchaser presses for a firm price quotation, will the price tendered be higher than a fixed price? The answer is not clear cut. While the contractor would like to add a cost contingency to compensate for the increased uncertainty, the ability to do so will depend upon the competitive pressure of the market place. In very competitive markets, the cost contingency may be zero and the risk of any future increases will be borne by the company without any 'buffer'.

❑ Fixed price contracts – variation of price formula

Some Government procurement organisations, perhaps unaware of the method-ology of Variation of Price (VOP) formula arrangements, insert very general price revision clauses in their longer term contracts, giving either party the right to re-negotiate the price after one year if, for any reason, it is no longer considered reasonable. Needless to say, this type of arrangement increases the level of risk to the purchasing organisation. Any increase (or decrease) will be dependent mainly on the strength of the evidence provided by the contractor and the negotiation skills of the buyer. The price amendment sought could be purely the result of reduced efficiency on the part of the contractor or cost increases which, with rea-sonable management, the contractor could have avoided. It might be very diffi-cult for the buyer to prove that this was the case. It would certainly be time con-suming to do so. As the negotiation would be taking place at a point when the increase was being sought by the current contractor, the negotiating power of the buyer would be small. The ultimate sanction is contract termination, but this would probably be a drastic solution from the purchaser's point of view, and so the price increase sought might reluctantly be met.

Variation of Price (VOP) arrangements formalise any price adjustments that may be made, and the basis of any changes is agreed at a sufficiently early stage for there to be adequate negotiating power for the purchaser to strike a fair deal. The essence of a VOP arrangement is that a proportion of the elements of the fixed price are varied in line with an appropriate labour or materials index, preferably at the end of the contract, so that the contractor is afforded some protection from cost increases. The aims of VOP clauses are:

(a) to give contractors a *measure* of protection against future increases in cost, whilst also preserving an incentive to

(b) contain costs, and in doing so

(c) to construct the simplest suitable arrangement.

The steps in establishing the VOP clause are basically as follows.

1 Procurement staff must satisfy themselves that the company's price break-down, the assessment of labour and materials requirements and of their costs and of other costs are broadly reasonable.

2 Where the contract price includes materials, finished parts or sub-contracts which, at the time of pricing, the contractor has already purchased or for which firm price quotations have been obtained, then these costs must be excluded from the VOP arrangements.

3 Whenever VOP arrangements are used, provision must be made for part of the price (frequently about 15 per cent) to be non-variable, as an incentive to the company to contain costs.

4 In respect of its tendered price, the company must state the 'base month' when the cost levels were current.

5 Adjustment of the fixed price must be based on the *average* movement of the indices over the appropriate periods.

6 Purchasing staff should normally use VOP clauses which provide for a single adjustment of the fixed price on completion of the contract, to minimise administrative costs.

7 The contract document should record sufficient information to make assessment of the payment due a straightforward arithmetical exercise.

The following is a typical example of the use of a VOP arrangement, following each of the steps outlined above. Assume that the price breakdown is as given in Figure 5.12. Thus, 51 per cent of the fixed price of £100,000.00 represents the labour element which will be varied in line with movements of the appropriate labour index. Similarly, 17 per cent of the fixed price of £100,000.00 represents the materials element which will be varied in line with the appropriate materials index.

To determine the effects of changes in the indices on the fixed price, at the end of the contract it is simply necessary to:

- calculate the *average* of each month's index figure for the period during which labour or materials costs were incurred

- then calculate the *average increase* of each month's figure in relation to the index for the 'base month' agreed with the contractor

- and finally, express this *average increase* in the form of a *percentage* of the 'base month' index.

		Labour (incl overheads and profit)	Raw materials (incl profit)	Total
1	Tendered price is: £100,000			
2	Breakdown of tendered price is;			
	– amount	£60,000	£40,000	£100,000
	- percentage of total	(60%)	(40%)	(100%)
3	Deduct the value of firm prices, say materials at £20,000, giving costs potentially subject to variation			
	- amount	£60,000	£20,000	—
	- percentage of total	(60%)	(20%)	
4	Deduct a non-variable element, say 15%, to give costs actually subject to variation, 'the variable element'			
	- amount	£51,000	£17,000	—
	- percentage of total	(51%)	(17%)	

Figure 5.12 Illustration of a variation of price arrangement

For example, taking some arbitrary figures, if the base month index for labour was 162.1 and the average of each month's index numbers over the period during whch labour costs were incurred was 179.7, then the average increase of the labour index, compared to the base month, would be 10.86%, ie:

$$179.7 - 162.1 = 17.6$$

This then needs to be expressed as a percentage of the base month:

$$(17.6/162.1) \times 100 = 10.86\%$$

Similarly, if the base month index for material was 143.9 and the average of each month's index numbers over the period during which material costs were incurred was 154.3, then the average increase of the materials index, compared to the base month, would be:

$$154.3 - 143.9 = 10.4$$

As a percentage of the base month index, this is:

$$(10.4 / 143.9) \times 100 = 7.22\%$$

Having calculated the percentage increases for labour and materials individually, it is now necessary to determine the adjustment to the overall tendered price of £100,000. This is achieved by applying the percentage average increase in each index to the appropriate portion of the contract price to which it relates and multiplying this by the fixed price. It is perhaps easier to illustrate than to describe. The formula is:

$$\text{Price adjustment} = \quad \text{fixed} \quad \times \quad \text{variable} \quad \times \quad \text{percentage average}$$
$$\text{price} \qquad \text{element} \qquad \text{increase of index}$$

Using the example in Figure 5.12, the labour price adjustment is given by:

$$£100,000 \times 51\% \times 10.86\% = £5,538.60$$

The materials price adjustment is given by:

$$£100,000 \times 17\% \times 7.22\% = £1,227.40$$

This gives a final price of

$$£100,000.00 + £5,538.60 + £1,227.40 = £106,766.00$$

For VOP purposes, the index numbers generally used in respect of labour are those contained in Table 5.3 of the *Employment Gazette*, a publication produced by the Department of Employment. Indices are also published in different sources to cover many individual categories of raw materials.

There is inevitably a measure of broad brush treatment in the use of indices. An assessment of the periods of expenditure on labour and material cannot be precise and the published indices may not fit exactly the type of labour or materials actually being employed. It is generally reasonable, however, to assume an even spread of expenditure over the identified periods, unless it is known that particular elements of cost will peak in particular periods.

Even if the indices available are not exactly the ones desired, VOP Formula contracts do offer the benefit of being more than an arbitrary periodic price review. In addition, the basis of the eventual price revision, the formula, is negotiated with the contractor at a stage when the purchasing department still has a fair degree of negotiating power.

Reference

Department of Employment *Employment Gazette*
London, Employment Department Group, Monthly

Chapter 6

Specifications

The successful outcome of a contract is mainly dependent on two procurement factors:

- abilities, capabilities and motivation of the contractor
- the specification.

The latter is the subject of this chapter. The contractor may deliver exactly what the purchaser asked for, but this will be of little consolation to the end users if the product delivered does not meet their requirements.

Describing the requirement

There are many ways of describing a requirement or part of a requirement. These include:

- commercial standards
- engineering drawings
- material
- method of manufacture
- brand names
- samples
- chemical analysis
- physical dimensions.

They are all, in their own way, examples of 'specifications'.

A good specification must be clear enough that the buyer and the seller are absolutely certain that the same product or service is being considered. It must also reflect the procurement considerations of market capability, materials availability and price.

Good specification writing is a skilled and time-consuming activity. Lack of attention to this phase in the procurement cycle inevitably leads to quality failures, strained buyer/supplier relationships and bitterness within the purchasing organisation. The most common mistakes made at the specification stage are probably:

- insufficient time allowed for completion
- over optimism on the part of the specification writers
- reluctance to challenge the glaringly obvious

- lack of involvement and consultatation with purchasing staff
- specifications which are too tight
- specifications which unnecessarily restrict competition
- insufficient awareness of the nature of the contract
- a 'mother hen' attitude on the part of the specification writers
- the use of unnecessary jargon
- use of functional or performance specification with inadequate suppliers.

Each of these will now be looked at in turn.

❏ Insufficient time allowed for completion

This mistake usually seems to be the result of an incomplete understanding of the full purpose and process of the specification phase. It needs to be appreciated that the specification will form the definitive description to ensure that potential suppliers:

- can know and understand what goods to supply, or what service to provide
- can estimate the resources required with reasonable accuracy
- can calculate the likely costs to be incurred in meeting the requirement
- can establish a price to be quoted.

This requires the specification to be clearly thought out. It may need to go through several drafts and require contributions from many interested parties. In its final form, given sufficient time for preparation, the specification will:

- be a clear, concise and unambiguous statement of the requirement
- be written in such a way that each tenderer has an equal opportunity to offer alternative products or services which meet the purchaser's need to take advantage of an innovative approach on the part of the contractor
- contain acceptance criteria against which goods or services offered may be evaluated
- comply with current legislation affecting the goods or service required
- comply with current legislation concerning public competition under the EC Procurement Directives, with no distortions to favour any supplier, product, process or source.

Much time and effort is required to compile a sound specification that can positively influence good value for money. Short-sighted attempts at cost savings at this critical stage, particularly in the early stages of procurement, insufficient consultation with end users and with others who have experience of purchasing the same or similar services and insufficient attention to detail, invariably lead to poorer value for money later on.

❑ Over-optimism on the part of the specification writers

In the real world, sustained high output with minimal quality failures may just be possible in certain, automated sectors of industry. However, wherever the human element is involved in supplying goods or providing services, output and quality can be subject to uncertainty unless there is adequate motivation and a systematic approach towards the elimination of quality failures.

It may be easy for the specification writers to *define* a certain level of output and failure rate, but it may be impossible for any potential supplier actually to *achieve* those performance criteria. Over-optimism on the part of the specification writers sometimes could stem from being out-of-touch with the market and current capabilities. Bringing expertise and experience together in a committee may help, but there is still a risk of:

- domination by one strong personality
- compromise between participants, where some people decline to challenge the ideas of others in return for acceptance of their own suggestions.

This situation is not helped by a reluctance to challenge the glaringly obvious.

❑ A reluctance to challenge the glaringly obvious

During the course of the preparation of a specification, the description, dimensions, tolerances and drawings are gradually developed from varying sources and brought together as a set of documents to become known as the specification. As this is happening, the status and credibility of the specification grows. People become committed to and defensive about their own ideas. The longer it is before the challenge the more committed and defensive they are likely to be. As specifications develop they may gather their own momentum and sense of importance, such that there is a danger that readers may convince themselves that what they contain must be right. There is no technical solution to this problem. To avoid it requires an openness, objectivity and a willingness to challenge and be challenged on the part of all those having some involvement with the specification.

❑ Lack of involvement of and consultation with purchasing staff

There is no doubt that the risk of contract problems at a later stage increases when the purchasing staff who will manage the purchase have not been involved from the outset. They need to be familiar with the specification to enable them to help develop a contract strategy and decide the method of purchase. In addition, it is they who will compile the contract conditions which need to complement the specification. Furthermore, as professional purchasing organisations are specialists in procurement and procurement law, they will be able to advise on any legal constraints which may affect the specification.

❑ Lack of involvement of other interested parties

Unfortunately, it is not all that unusual to hear the 'customer' describe the goods which they have received or the service with which they have been provided as not what was needed. Generally speaking, in Government, they recognise the policy of openness in competition and the continuing search for value for money in Government procurement. They accept, perhaps reluctantly, that they won't necessarily be provided with what they would ideally *want*. However, they do have reasonable expectations that they will be provided with what they *need*, this being one of the objectives of the procurement organisation.

When failures of this type arise, they invariably stem from a lack of consultation and involvement at the specification stage. Nearly all specifications are compromises of one sort or another, and it is only from early consultation and negotiation with all interested parties that the likelihood of developing an acceptable compromise is increased.

It is the natural tendency of the client to say of a specification:

> it doesn't describe what we want,

The specification writer will then say,

> it's the best that you'll get.

The purchaser is often in the best position to bring the two parties together to identify what would actually meet the organisation's need. Compromises can be worked out when the various aspects of the problem are understood by the parties who should be involved.

All of this increases the time required to complete the specification process, but the value of potential money savings at this stage is likely far to outweigh the effort required.

❑ Specifications which are too tight

A common misunderstanding about specifications is that they should be very 'tight,' the thinking being that such specifications will surely provide the correct good or service. There is sometimes a tendency in compiling specifications to demand the best or to tighten things up to be on the safe side. When safety matters really are under consideration, the 'best possible' may be the only sensible choice.

However, specifications which are too tight result in less choice and less competition, because:

- a number of readily available acceptable products or services may not be compliant
- the number of potential suppliers with the sufficient capability may be few.

Less competition in itself poses a risk to value for money and unnecessary precision, by increasing a supplier's costs and the number of rejects, will lead to higher prices in the tender. Clarity and lack of ambiguity are important, not tightness *per se*.

Determining *acceptable* tolerances is another of those areas where consultation with and involvement of the appropriate parties is vital.

❑ Specifications which unnecessarily restrict competition

The tight specification is a particular example of a specification which unnecessarily restricts competition. Other examples of specifications which unnecessarily restrict competition are those which:

- are written around a specific product or service, and slanted towards few suppliers, thus reducing or precluding competition
- which are too prescriptive, and over-specify, not allowing potential suppliers sufficient scope to use their available expertise
- which do not allow potential suppliers to offer alternative, innovative solutions that give better value for money.

The daily press much enjoy publicising requirements which have been over-specified. In recent years there have been the cases of the purchase of ketchup by a US Government Agency that was required to pour at no more than 0.00522 mph, and the vacuum flask for pilot's coffee which was required to work in temperatures down to –95 degrees celsius, long after the pilot had more pressing concerns than a cup of coffee!

It is usually fairly easy to spot the over-specified requirement because the number of technical details will swamp the functional and performance characteristics. Obviously, some requirements need to be more technically specified than others, but the danger is that their inclusion may actually limit the functional and performance characteristics which can be achieved.

It is not only the technical aspects of a requirement which may be over- specified. If the procurement organisation is able to remain flexible about the provision of a service, for example, when and how it is delivered, significant cost savings may be achieved by a potential supplier. These savings can then be passed on to the purchasing department by way of a lower price or more coverage at the same price. So, wherever possible, the potential suppliers should not be discouraged by the nature of the specification from using their own expertise to propose innovative solutions and share the benefits of value for money improvements.

❏ Insufficient awareness of the nature of the contract

Recent public sector procurement issues such as 'market testing' and 'contracting out' have made all public servants far more aware of the meaning of the word 'contract'. Up until the last five years or so, however, it was not unusual to encounter an attitude, outside the procurement section, which implied that the relationship between the public purchaser and the supplier was believed to be largely altruistic. The supplier was expected to do as they were told, for nothing, as changes in the specification ebbed and flowed from the purchaser.

Attitudes have now changed, but there will always potentially be a lack of adequate legal awareness as more and more staff become involved in some contractual aspect of their work, for example, when working with consultants or becoming involved with drawing up specifications. A commercial frame of mind has to be adopted, so that people are aware of the potential costs associated with, say:

- contract amendments required resulting from inappropriate specifications
- extra-contractual claims from contractors to cover costs arising from faulty or inaccurate specifications.

❏ A 'mother hen' attitude on the part of the specification writers

Apart from the in-built resistance to change of any specification as it develops, those involved with writing the specification frequently take on fierce maternal instincts when their 'baby' is threatened in any way. Even reasonable challenges can be fought off with little reference to logic and much use of emotion. Once again this highlights the need for the procurement section to become involved at the earliest possible point and the near futility of attempting to achieve anything other than the most minor of changes at a late stage.

❏ The use of unnecessary jargon

There sometimes seems to be a fear among specification writers, particularly the inexperienced, that simple and easy-to-understand specifications look inadequate. It is not that they are really *believed* to be inadequate, but they just look that way. So, to make the specification appear more impressive, it is compiled using plenty of jargon, and simple language is made more complex by the use of long sentences and big words. There seems to be a fear among those who draft contracts. They need their 'whereinafters' and 'heretofores', but do such words really help anyone else?

Clear specifications greatly increase the chances of a successful outcome, both at the tender and contract stages because they encourage the widest competition and because they increase the level of understanding of the rights and obligations of both parties to the contract. For a specification to be clear it should be simple enough for a layperson to understand, and so should:

- use simple language
- not use jargon
- be concise but remain clear
- have initials, symbols and terms defined
- be set out logically
- avoid the risk of contradiction by
- describing each aspect of the requirement in one place only.

❏ Use of functional or performance specifications with inadequate suppliers

Functional and performance specifications are generally easier to prepare than, say, detailed technical specifications and so use less resources. As the name implies, functional specifications define the *purpose* of the requirement and describe *what* is to be achieved. The method of achieving the end result is left to the potential suppliers. Similarly, performance specifications define the required output, but not how it should be achieved by the potential suppliers.

The use of such types of specification helps achieve value for money by harnessing the ideas and initiative of the suppliers. However it can lead to potential problems if inadequate supplier appraisal has been conducted. This is because the eventual contractor will assume complete responsibility for designing and making the product, and contractors who are not fully capable may not be able to achieve the outcomes promised at the tender stage.

It is true that the specification is at the heart of the contract and that success or failure can hinge upon the right approach to its compilation. However, this last point is a timely reminder that even an appropriate and good specification requires an appropriate and good supplier for a high probability of procurement success.

Chapter 7

Terms and conditions of contract

The phrase 'contract terms and conditions' is invariably used in everyday language between buyers and sellers. These terms may be either:

- express, or
- implied.

If express, it means that they are expressly agreed between the parties to the contract. They may be implied by:

- being incorporated into the contract by some statutory legislation, for example, the Sale of Goods Act (1979) or the Supply of Goods and Services Act (1982)
- by previous dealings between the parties
- by trade usage.

Conditions and warranties

It is more precise to refer to contract terms described above as 'conditions and warranties'. The difference between a condition and a warranty is as follows. In its usual meaning, a condition is a major term, of vital importance, that goes to the root of the contract. If a seller is in breach of a contract condition, the buyer has the right to:

- reject the goods
- treat the contract as at an end, and
- claim damages from the seller.

A warranty, however, is a collateral term, that is, connected but aside from the main purpose of the contract. The seller's breach of a warranty allows the buyer to:

- claim for damages, but
- does not release the buyer from any contractual obligations.

Practically speaking, a condition is a major term and a warranty is a minor term, (unless subject to any clear contrary intention).

❑ Whose conditions and warranties?

An underlying objective of all professional purchasers, whether in the public or private sector, is to achieve the best overall deal for their employing organisation, in the long term as well as the short term. This will mean that not only will the goods or services procured meet the contract specification, but also the other 'half' of the contract, the terms and conditions, will be appropriately enforced.

In considering the legal aspects of contracting at chapter 3, it was stated that commercial sellers, given the choice, would prefer to contract on their own terms and conditions, carefully compiled to maximise the commercial opportunities and minimise the commercial risk to the supplier. Similarly, committed public sector purchasers would strive to achieve the best deal to meet their *organisation's* objectives, by ensuring that any contracts formed were to their terms and conditions.

❑ Seller's terms and conditions

If public sector purchasers were to contract on the basis of the seller's terms and conditions, they would increase the level of risk to their employer, sometimes significantly so. This can be illustrated by examining a supplier's conditions of sale. They will often be quite surprising and leave the public sector buyer in no doubt as to whose conditions would best protect the public body's contractual position. As an example, the following terms and conditions, while extreme, might reflect a seller's viewpoint.

CONDITIONS OF SALE

1 Price

The seller reserves the right by notice given at any time before delivery, to vary the price of the goods if there is any increase in the total cost of such goods to the seller arising from any cause beyond the seller's control.

2 Merchantable quality and fitness for purpose

All warranties and conditions, express and implied, statutory and otherwise, as to the quality of the goods or their fitness for any purpose are hereby excluded.

3 Liabilities

The seller shall not be liable for:

(a) failure to perform any obligation hereunder if such failure was caused by circumstances beyond the seller's control or,

(b) delay howsoever caused in performing any obligations here-under.

4 Ownership and risk

The ownership of goods delivered under the contract shall be transferred to the buyer when the buyer has met all that is owing to the seller on whatever grounds. The risk of damage, deterioration or destruction shall pass on delivery and the buyer shall insure against such risk. Where goods are delivered by an independent carrier, delivery to the carrier shall be deemed to be delivery to the buyer.

Quite clearly, and perhaps naturally, the above selection of conditions of sale are looking after the seller's interests. Amongst other things, Clause 2 seeks to exclude the buyer's rights of merchantable quality and fitness for purpose under Sections 14 and 15 of the Sale of Goods Act (1979). Although it is often assumed that such a condition of sale is 'illegal' in some way, it is, in fact, only in consumer contracts that liability for breach of these statutory rights cannot be excluded or restricted by reference to any contractual term. This is provided for under Section 2 of the Unfair Contract Terms Act (1977).

This same Act describes the activities of a Government department as a business, not as a consumer. Because of this, the liabilities relating to merchantable quality, fitness for purpose and nearly all of the other terms implied by the Sale of Goods Act *can* be excluded by the seller, but only in so far as the term satisfies the requirement of reasonableness as defined by the Unfair Contract Terms Act.

Obviously, there are far better ways of spending public money than contracting on the basis of a supplier's terms and conditions which severely limit the rights of the buying organisation. This point is valid even *if* it can be later demonstrated, at great expense of time and effort, that the limitations *were* unreasonable and therefore invalid. Examination of a seller's terms, usually serves to emphasise how vital it is to safeguard the public sector's rights by ensuring that all contracts are formed on the basis of the purchaser's terms and conditions (with the exception, perhaps, of very low value, low risk purchases). The purchaser must take great care when contracting with the supplier to ensure that this is the case.

❏ Offer and acceptance revisited

In chapter 3, it was seen that, unless otherwise stated, a simple contract can be made:

* expressly, in writing
* expressly, by word of mouth

- implied by the action of the parties
- any combination of these three methods.

Consider the following series of events:

(a) a Government department offered to purchase some goods on its own terms and conditions

(b) the supplier responded with a despatch notice referring to *their* terms and conditions; this was filed, and the goods subsequently arrived

(c) the goods were unpacked and taken into use by the department.

It is probable, given the brief details above, that a contract had been created by the department's implied acceptance at (c) of the supplier's counter-offer made at (b). Therefore, quite unintentionally, a contract had been created on the supplier's terms and conditions. Furthermore, it was quite possible that no one in the department had even fully read them!

❑ Seller's guarantees

It is quite common for inexperienced buyers to look for and feel comforted by a seller's guarantee. However, it is not at all unusual for suppliers of goods or services to provide guarantees which protect the seller more than the buyer in the event of a quality failure. Something along the following lines might be offered in a contract for goods:

Guarantee

For the period of twelve calendar months, the seller will repair or replace at no charge to the buyer, any components, assemblies or sub-assemblies of the seller's manufacture which fail due to faulty materials or workmanship. The liability of the company under this guarantee shall be limited to thevalue of the components, assemblies or subassemblies replaced or repaired.

An inexperienced buyer may be content just to see that the goods were guaranteed for twelve months and read no further than the heading and the first line. However, exactly what is the benefit of this contract term to the buyer? Very little, in fact. Its main purpose is to limit the seller's liability and thereby protect the seller from any claim from the buyer for a consequential loss arising from the use of the goods. For example, under this 'guarantee' the supplier of a defective office machine which causes £1 million of fire damage to the buying department is liable only for the repair or replacement of the defective parts! In this case, and in many others, the buyer is better protected by the Sale of Goods Act than a seller's guarantee.

❏ Systematic approach

Quite clearly, the objective of purchasers is to contract on their organisation's terms and conditions. To be confident that these apply, a detailed, systematic approach to each 'legal' phase of the purchase is required. At each phase there should be:

- certainty about which party is making the offer
- certainty about what the offer contains, (it should include the appropriate purchaser's terms and conditions which will form part of the contract created when the unqualified acceptance of that offer is made)
- extreme care when making or receiving counter offers
- certainty about which party made the unqualified acceptance (and of what), thereby forming the contract
- certainty about exactly *when* the contract was created so that there is no doubt that the purchaser's terms and conditions applied.

With this approach, there should be little question about whose terms and conditions formed the basis of the contract, and greater certainty that the contract is based upon the terms and conditions of the purchasing organisation.

Government terms and conditions of contract

Depending upon the nature of the contract, the terms and conditions may need to cover many issues, clearly stating the rights and obligations of the parties in relation to each issue. Furthermore, they would need to address situations anticipated by the purchaser, and, once again, clearly state the rights and obligations of the parties to the contract should such situations arise in practice.

Practically all significant Government contracts contain terms and conditions taken from or based upon *Standard Conditions of Government Contracts for Stores Purchases - Form GC/Stores/1* (April 1979). This is particularly true of the larger departments or those with a long history of purchasing. The front cover of *GC/Stores/1* states that:

> This Booklet of Conditions of Government Contracts has been adopted by the principal Government Purchasing Departments for the purpose of ensuring uniformity of Contract Conditions between themselves and Contractors, and also to achieve economy in time and paper.

Tender and Contract documents will, as far as these conditions are concerned, contain only a reference to the Booklet numbers of the applicable Conditions together with any special conditions or amendments to the Standard Conditions.

The Booklet is in two parts. All of Part I will normally be used by all Departments. Conditions in Part II may be used as appropriate.

The existence of the *GC/Stores/1 Booklet*, and its availability to tenderers and contractors, makes it possible for purchasing departments to make easy reference in contract and tender documents to the Standard Conditions it contains. By simply referring to the Booklet edition number and the Standard Condition number, an enormous saving in time and paper can be achieved compared to inclusion of the full text in a tender or contract document.

Apart from economy in time and paper, another important benefit of standard conditions is that they help to ensure a uniformity of approach, in terms of policy and practice across departments in their dealings with the private sector. In addition, over time, the language and interpretation of standard conditions has become recognised, helping to ensure a clear understanding between the parties of each other's rights and obligations under the contract.

The terms and conditions in *GC/Stores/1* were negotiated by a working party of the Purchase and Sale of Goods Sub-committee, under the authority of the Treasury's Procurement Policy Committee. These negotiations involved full discussions with the Contracts Panel of the Confederation of British Industry (CBI), who in turn consulted the relevant Trade Associations for their views.

Although the language of the terms and conditions contained in *GC/Stores/1* is not 'easy', they are well-tried and familiar to many, both in the public and private sectors. One possible reason why they have not been used across all departments could simply be from ignorance of their existence, especially in those cases where private sector advisors have been employed who had no experience of their practical use in Government contracting. Another reason is that the terms and conditions in *GC/Stores/1* may have been perceived as being unnecessarily complicated for the straightforward, relatively low value purchases which some departments regularly make. Whatever the reason, the outcome is that there is less uniformity and economy than there might have been. In addition, there are some poorer Government contracts in existence as a result of using less than adequate 'home grown' terms and conditions, or even worse, apparently none at all.

Other booklets of standard government conditions are available, such as:

- *GC/Works/1 (Edition 2 September 1977) – General Conditions of Government Contracts for Building and Civil Engineering Works*
- *GC/Works 2 (Edition 2 January 1980) – General Conditions of Government Contracts for Minor Building and Civil Engineering Works*
- *GC/Sales (Edition, November 1978) – Standard Conditions for Sale of Goods. C1001 (October 1985)– General Conditions of Government Contracts for Building, Civil Engineering, Mechanical and Electrical Small Works.*

For information, the table of contents of *GC/Stores/1* is shown in Figures 7.1a and 7.1b. Note that some sections are currently not used; this accounts for the missing numbers.

STANDARD CONDITIONS OF GOVERNMENT CONTRACTS

FOR STORES PURCHASES

TABLE OF CONTENTS

Part I

1 Interpretations, etc	13 Value Added Tax
2 Specifications, etc	14 Default
3 Alteration of Specifications, Plans, Drawings, Patterns, and Samples	15 Bankruptcy, etc
4 Inspection	16 Racial Discrimination
5 Acceptance Marks	17 Fair Wages, etc
6 Packages	18 Transfer and Sub-letting
7 Delivery	19 Customs Duty Drawback
8 Rendering of Bills	20 Corrupt Gifts and Payments of Commission
9 Recovery of Sums Due	21 Official Secrets Act
10 Progress Reports	24 Rejection
11 Issues of Government Property	25 Acceptance
12 Loss of or Damage to the Articles, etc	

Figure 7.1a Contents of GC/Stores/1–Part I

PART II

29	Law (English)
29a	Law (Scottish)
30	Arbitration (English Law)
30a	Arbitration (Scottish Law)
31	Use of Documents, Information, etc
32a	Patents, etc
32b	Contracts for Defence Material subject to Defence Contracts Act 1958–Agreements in Relation to Technical Information
36	Labour Conditions (Made-up Textiles, Equipment, etc)
41	Delivery under Warrants or Orders
42	Materials Requirement
43	Price Fixing
44	Variation of Price (Wages)
45	Variation of Price (Materials)
46	Variation of Price (Sub-contracts)
47	Variation of Price (General Provisions)

48	Availability of Information
49	Vesting
50	References to the Review Board of Questions arising under the Contract
51	References to the Review Board of Questions arising in Relation to Relevant Sub-contracts
52	References to the Review Board of Questions arising in Relation to Relevant Parts of the Work placed with Subsidiaries
53	Pricing on Ascertained Costs
55	Damage to Government Property
56	Break
59	Security Measures
60	Tests

Figure 7.1b Contents of GC/Stores/1 --Part II

It would be highly unlikely for any government contract to be adequately drafted using only the conditions in *GC/Stores/1*, and so there is always a need for a department to use its own standard terms and conditions as a supplement. The aim, though, is to keep these additions to a practical minimum. To aid understanding, and as a basis of comparison if similar alternatives are used, all of the conditions from Part I of *GC/Stores/1* are described in Annex A, some in detail, as they (or similar alternatives) are generally used in all Government contracts. Some of the conditions from Part II are described as well, but others are omitted because they are only appropriate for certain types of very high value contract and are mainly used, therefore, by only one or two departments.

❏ Liquidated damages

The parties to a contract may make specific provisions regarding a sum of money to be paid by way of compensation in the event of a breach occurring eg late delivery. If that sum is a *genuine pre-estimate of loss*, this is termed 'liquidated damages', and the courts will allow recovery of this sum *whether or not this sum represents the actual loss suffered.*

However, if the sum incorporated into the contract is *not* a genuine pre-estimate of loss, but is there to threaten or terrorise the contractor to meet the requirements of the contract, then this is termed a 'penalty' and the courts will not enforce the recovery of such a sum, but instead, they will fix damages based on the actual loss suffered. Whether or not the sum incorporated into the contract condition represents a penalty or liquidated damages will, in the event of dispute, be decided by the courts. This is so even if the parties to the contract have designated the sum in the condition as a penalty or liquidated damages.

❏ *Force majeure*

Force majeure is the name given to a contract term that relieves contractors of the consequences of events beyond their control. Suppliers may seek the purchaser's agreement of a specific provision in a contract which would preclude a claim for damages in certain circumstances. War, Acts of God, strikes and lock-outs are common examples. It is quite usual for Government departments to resist the inclusion of such clauses on the grounds that the Government department would act reasonably, on a case-by-case basis, if the circumstances arose. There is always a risk with a wide-ranging *force majeure* clause that it will be used to the seller's advantage in circumstances that weren't envisaged by the purchaser.

Reference

Form GC/Stores/1 (April 1979) *Standard Conditions of Government Contracts for Stores Purchases*, London, HMSO.

Chapter 8

Payment terms

In dealing with suppliers, professional purchasers should ensure that the manufacturer of a product or provider of a service has the means necessary to carry on their business. This was considered in chapter 4 as an element of 'supplier appraisal'. One of those means is 'working capital', namely the money necessary to meet current expenses, such as the payment of wages and the cost of materials, while production is in progress but not completed.

There are a number of ways in which the working capital necessary for the execution of contracts could be provided. These are:

- the responsibility could be left entirely with the contractors, to supply the working capital from their own resources or by borrowing commercially
- the purchaser could accept the responsibility, in whole or in part, by:
    - (i) providing a loan to the contractor,
    - (ii) making part-payment in advance when the contract is made, or
    - (iii) by progress or stage payments made during the course of the contract.

The general rule adopted by Government is, as far as practicable, to place the onus on the contractor to fund the contract, payment being made when the product or service is delivered and accepted. Its view is that industry should look to the banking system for its short-term finance, and that purchasers should choose to deal only with companies with sufficient financial resources to complete any contracts awarded to them. This is a perfectly reasonable view for any public or private sector purchasing organisation to take.

However, it is recognised, particularly with high value, long duration contracts, involving exceptional amounts of working capital, that some special provision may be made to reduce the level of working capital required. In doing so, the purchaser should recognise the real value to the supplier of any form of special provision. Any help with a supplier's cash flow is a valuable concession and so, as with any concession, something of value should be received in return.

Interim payments

In certain circumstances some form of interim payment, a payment prior to delivery or completion, may be considered necessary. The use of such payments varies in detail between one Government department and another, but the principles involved are the same. They are associated with long duration, high value contracts because it is on these that the contractor will face the biggest working capital burden, perhaps facing a year or more before work is completed and payment of the (substantial) price is authorised against the invoice.

❑ The advantages and disadvantages of interim payments

Before considering the workings of two types of interim payment in detail, it is worth reflecting on the advantages and disadvantages of making interim payments in general, from both the purchaser's and the contractor's point of view. Figure 8.1 tabulates some of the considerations.

	Possible advantages	Possible disadvantages
P u r c h a s e r	– more choice – lower prices	– less incentive to complete – less incentive to deliver – more work to administer – cost to Government
C o n t r a c t o r	– eases cash flow – interest free loan	– more work to administer

Figure 8.1 The advantages and disadvantages of interim payments

Generally speaking, there is very little, if anything, to be gained by the purchaser from the use of interim payments. In theory, lower prices should automatically result from the reduction in the firm's capital employed, and the reduction in the contractor's need to borrow commercially. Central Government should normally be able to borrow on more favourable terms than a private firm. However, there is no guarantee that these savings will be passed on in full, so that the price reduction may amount to less than the costs of funding it. In a competitive tender situation, the potential use of interim payments may widen the choice of interested suppliers, particularly for very high value and long duration contracts. However, there is an increased risk of attracting tenderers with insufficient financial resources to carry out the work.

A requirement for contractors to finance the contract from their own working capital, or by borrowing commercially, can be a healthy stimulus to concentrate on the work in hand, leading to timely and efficient completion. Conversely, if a public sector purchaser takes too relaxed an attitude to the use of interim payments, forgetting to question what they are costing and what concessions are obtained in return, they could become perceived by all concerned as the norm. Contractors could thereby be encouraged to demand increasingly generous interim payment arrangements.

There are essentially two types of interim payment which may be appropriate for long duration, high value contracts. They are:

- stage payments
- progress payments.

Stage payments

As the name implies, these are payments

- made at *very specific stages* of the work carried out under the contract
- that are *clearly defined* in the contract schedule
- which *relate to effort expended and progress* satisfactorily achieved.

They are generally used in conjunction with firm price or fixed price contracts. When the specific stage has been met, a percentage of the contract price is paid. Where necessary, several stages can be used but care must be taken to ensure that the contractor always has sufficient incentive to complete the work and deliver it. This means that:

- the percentage paid must never exceed the percentage of effort expended
- the final stage must be large enough to be significant, so that the contractor is motivated to complete this job rather than move to another lucrative one.

Withholding 20 per cent or 25 per cent of the price is common, anything less than this could constitute a risk.

Consider a very simplified example of a typical stage payment scheme, in this case for the modification and repair of an aircraft. This is shown in Figure 8.2.

Contract requirement	Firm price each
Repair and modify aircraft to specification	£200,000
Stage payment scheme	
Stage identified	**% of firm price paid**
1 All contract repairs completed and signed-off	45%
2 All contract modifications fitted and signed-off	65%
3 Electrical systems operational	75%

Figure 8.2 Example of a stage payment scheme

The intention with a stage payment scheme is to match payments as far as possible with physical progress. For example, in Figure 8.2, having identified stage 1 as an appropriate point to make a payment, the percentage of the contractor's total effort required to reach it is estimated. If this is 45 per cent, this percentage is used to apportion the payment of the price. The aim is that it should take *at least* 45 per cent of the contractor's effort under the contract to complete this stage satisfactorily, whereupon 45 per cent of the contract price would be paid. The same approach is followed for the remaining stages. In addition, because the payment at the final stage is set at 75 per cent, there should be sufficient incentive for the contractor to complete *all* of the work under the contract, so as to avoid delays in acceptance, at which point the balance of the price would be paid.

In compiling a stage payment scheme, specialist advice would often need to be sought by the purchaser to estimate the level of effort required to reach the stage defined. A contractor's own assessment might possibly be calculated to reward them in advance of effort being expended.

❑ Progress payments

Some Government departments do not distinguish between stage payments and progress payments, usually because they use only one type, stage payments, and commonly refer to them as either stage payments or progress payments.

However, one or two departments need to distinguish between:

- stage payments, used in a priced contract with clearly defined stages, and
- progress payments, used when stages are impossible to define and a firm price or fixed price is not practicable.

Progress payments usually relate in some way to a contractor's costs. An example may be a monthly payment of a proportion of the contractor's direct and indirect costs properly incurred in execution of the work under the contract. The inherent risk with this type of interim payment is that paying a proportion of the contractor's costs does not necessarily promise progress under the contract. At worst the contractor could be incurring significant costs, possibly inefficiently, and achieving nothing. Progress payments of this sort would therefore be used in conjunction with a contract requirement for 'technical' progress meetings with the contractor to accompany the submission by the contractor of monthly or quarterly financial reports. Progress payments of this type raise the need for technical and financial monitoring. Progress payments of a pre-specified amount at regular intervals are generally a recipe for disaster. There is clear risk that payments could precede expenditure of effort such that money is 'owed' by the contractor to the purchaser, an unsatisfactory position for any purchasing organisation, whether in the public or private sector.

❏ Advance payments

It can be only too easy for bad habits to develop in a purchasing organisation, particularly where there is a rapid turnover of staff and adequate training is neglected. One such area is the practice of making advance payments, that is payments in advance of any work being undertaken, perhaps in return for a price discount. We have seen that the risks involved in making 'legitimate' forms of interim payment can be high, as well as having costs associated with them. Therefore, handing over taxpayer's money to a contractor in return for nothing, except a price discount, does not say much for the purchaser's negotiation technique. Unfortunately, advance payments have become 'standard practice' in certain sectors of industry but generally not in areas where Government purchasing staff are involved. As we have seen, it is not the Government's policy to act as a source of loan finance for contractors and, consequently, it is no surprise that prior Treasury approval is required for advance payments to be made, and this may only exceptionally be given where a financial appraisal has been conducted to establish a value for money case. Because of the risks and costs involved, advance payments are anathema to the professional purchaser, in both the private and public sectors; they should never be made by a really skilled negotiator.

Ownership of assets

The term 'property' is commonly used by lawyers to signify title or ownership. Generally speaking, the transfer of ownership from the seller to the buyer is referred to as:

the passing of property.

It is not always appreciated that it is possible for ownership to pass from the contractor without the buyer being in possession of the goods. It is vital for the purchaser to know whether or not ownership of the goods has passed from the seller because:

- as a general rule, (unless otherwise agreed,) the risk of accidental loss or damage passes with the property
- if the seller becomes bankrupt it must be decided in whom the ownership rests
- once the ownership has passed, the seller can sue the buyer for the price.

❏ Without interim payments

It is a basic requirement for Government contracts that, in general, goods or services are not paid for until they are received, this being a sensible safeguard when spending taxpayer's money. In contracts where no payment is made until the goods are received or the service has been provided, contract conditions should ensure that ownership and risk transfer to Government when and where delivery is made. This point is covered, for example, by *Standard Conditions of Government Contracts,* specifically Standard Condition 7, covering 'Delivery', and Standard Condition 12, covering 'Loss or Damage to the Articles' (see chapter 7).

It has been recognised, though, that interim payments are made in certain circumstances, with the result that money is handed over *prior* to delivery or completion, a high risk arrangement. To minimise the risk in these situations, an essential condition to the granting of such payments is that ownership of each article, component part, raw materials, and so on, should rest with the Government department from the outset. A typical contract condition is Standard Condition 49, (SC49) on 'Vesting'. Clause (1) of this is shown in Figure 8.3. There is no intention with SC49 that the value of vested material, etc, should be matched against payments made, neither does the vesting depend on any interim payment actually being made.

Standard Condition 49

Clause 1

Subject to the following provisions of this Condition –

(a) each Article as it is constructed together with its component parts and equipment so far as incorporated therein, and

(b) all materials and other things whatsoever which the Contractor shall acquire or allocate for incorporation in any of the Articles, shall vest in and become the absolute property of the Authority, as from the time the construction of the Article begins or the materials or things are so acquired or allocated and shall thenceforth be in the possession of the Contractor for the sole purpose of completing the Articles and delivering them when completed to the Authority, and shall not be within the ownership, control or disposition of the Contractor.

Figure 8.3 Interim payments – vesting

Another risk of making interim payments, which is also addressed by SC49, is that a stage payment, 75 per cent for example, may be erroneously authorised because a partially completed product, seen at the contractor's works, is in fact for delivery to a different customer of the company. The Government's part finished article may only be at the 50 per cent stage! Clause 3 of SC49 requires that, from the outset, the contractor either marks or clearly identifies everything, the property of which is vested in the Authority. This Clause is mainly to ensure that, should the company go bankrupt, the things owned by the Authority are easily recovered.

If SC49 ensures that the property has passed to the Authority from the outset, it is also necessary to ensure that the risk of accidental loss or damage *remains* with the contractor. Otherwise the general rule in law, that risk passes with property, will apply. This safeguard is typically provided through SC12, 'Loss or Damage to the Articles', which makes the contractor responsible for making good any loss or damage at any time before delivery, even if property has already passed under SC49.

This is not an easy area to understand at first sight, but it is a vital one if the Government purchaser is to protect the Government's rights and manage the risks under contract.

Prompt payment of bills

Government departments are, in the main, prompt payers of their suppliers, delays arising mainly where invoice documents or validation certificates are not complete. In many parts of the private sector slow payment of bills has been used as another method of funding a company's working capital, with disastrous cash-flow consequences, particularly for smaller firms. Some leading companies have now signed up to a code of practice which requires prompt payment of suppliers.

The response of the Government to the scale of the problem of slow payment was to announce in the 1992 Budget statement the introduction of new procedures to ensure prompt payment by Government contractors to their subcontractors. From April 1992 clauses were introduced into all Government contracts to ensure that Government best practice became the norm in the private sector, the intention being that payment by contractors to their own suppliers was made within 30 days. An example of a typical clause for the purchase of goods or services is as follows:

> Where the Contractor enters a subcontract with a supplier or contractor for the purpose of performing the Contract, the Contractor shall cause a term to be included in such subcontract which requires payment to be made to the supplier or contractor within a specified period not exceeding 30 days from receipt of a valid invoice as defined by the subcontract requirements.

The wording used for works and construction contracts is different, but the principle is the same. If a contractor has *performed poorly* under a contract as a result of failing to pay their subcontractors promptly, this is a factor which departments would take into account in awarding subsequent contracts.

❏ The value of money

The lengths to which a supplier will go to obtain some form of contract payment, (and the earlier the better,) and the measures which some unscrupulous buyers will take to avoid paying anything until the last possible moment, highlights the real value which the use of money confers. This value is often not recognised by those in the public sector because they are remote from the problems of cash flow (treasury) management. Their main concern is the position at the end of the financial year, (31 March,) and there is no benefit to their budgets if payments are made in December rather than November or vice versa.

Government rightly pays its contract bills speedily once work has been validated or invoices received, but it also rightly seeks to avoid making unnecessary progress or stage payments as this leads to higher Exchequer financing costs than payments made later. If a substantial interim payment is being considered, a financial appraisal is required to calculate the 'value' of the monetary payments to the supplier and the cost to Government. Knowing the value and cost of the interim payment 'concession' allows a view to be taken of the level of price reduction which should be sought from the supplier in return.

Reference

Standard Conditions of Government Contracts for Stores Purchases, London, HMSO.

Chapter 9

Profit formula contracts

Most Government procurement staff do not know, and do not need to know, the level of profit achieved by contractors when carrying out work under Government contracts. This is because, wherever possible, competitive tendering will have been used as the preferred method of procurement. When competition is effective, the appropriate level of profit for each contract price is set essentially by the market.

However, not all Government procurement staff have the luxury of an effective competitive market. They may be buying complex equipment for which there is only one supplier. Furthermore, the Government department in which they work may be the only customer for that equipment. In this situation, the supplier naturally wants to maximise the level of profit achieved under the contract whereas the Government department wants to limit the profit to a more reasonable level. The profit formula has been developed to reduce the uncertainty about the appropriate level of profit for contracts awarded in these non-competitive markets.

The profit formula agreement

On 26 February 1968, the Chief Secretary to the Treasury announced to Parliament that the Government had reached agreement with industry for dealing with non-competitive Government contracts, and that a profit formula would be used. The aim of this formula was to give contractors a fair return on their capital employed, (see chapter 4), that is, a return equal on average to the overall return earned by British industry. Profit formula contracts have been used by Government since that date for high value requirements which could only be met from a non-competitive market.

The rate of profit deemed to give a fair return on a contractor's capital employed is calculated by an independent body called the Review Board for Government Contracts, taking into account the views of the Confederation of British Industry, other interested trade associations and the Government. The Board examines the profitability of a reference group of relevant companies in the UK, and sets a target rate of return on capital employed. As a result of the Seventh General Review (1993), the historic cost rate of return is currently 19.45 per cent on capital employed for risk contracts, and the semi-current cost accounting rate of return is 13.85 per cent on capital employed for non-risk contracts. In chapter 4 capital employed was defined as:

> share capital + loan capital + reserves

or, alternatively, as:

> fixed assets + current assets - current liabilities.

Risk contracts are those where the contractor is at risk of making a loss on the contract. This is the situation where a price is agreed at an early point of the contract, either before any work has started or as soon the parties are able during the course of the contract. A loss would then be incurred if the contractor's costs exceeded the contract price. Non-risk contracts are those on which the contractor cannot make a loss because the contract price will be based upon the contractor's costs incurred to complete the contract requirement. The non-risk profit rate is applied to those costs.

The profit formula is intended not only to give a fair return on, and provide for, the risk to the capital employed in the business, but also to reward and encourage the efficiency of the contractor. In order to meet these two objectives, the formula is a two-part device comprising:

(i) a capital-based element which varies with the ratio (CP:CE) of the contractor's cost of production to capital employed

(ii) a cost-based element which is constant.

❑ Using the profit formula

To calculate the percentage profit to be applied to a particular contractor's costs, whether estimated (for a risk contract), or ascertained (for a non-risk contract), it is necessary to know the contractor's CP:CE ratio and the profit formula currently in use. The most recent (1993) historic cost profit formula applicable to risk contracts is:

> 9.7% on capital employed + 4.6% on costs of production

On the basis of an average CP:CE ratio of 2.12:1, this formula gives the appropriate reward of 19.45 per cent on capital employed, calculated as follows:

> 9.7% on CE + (4.6% X 2.12) on CE = 19.45% on CE

In the calculation above, the profit rate in the second part of the formula has been converted from a rate expressed as a percentage of costs of production to a rate expressed as a percentage of capital employed, by multiplying the 4.6 per cent on costs of production by the CP:CE ratio to give 9.75 per cent. When this figure is added to the 9.7 per cent on CE from the first part of the formula, a total return of 19.45 per cent on capital employed is obtained.

This calculation demonstrates that, using the formula, the target rate of return on capital employed for a risk contract is achieved by a contractor with an average CP:CE ratio of 2.12:1. In day-to-day pricing situations, profit formula contracts are priced on the basis of either estimated or ascertained costs. A profit rate expressed in terms of a return on capital employed is, therefore, not of much use. What is required is a profit rate, derived from the formula, but expressed in terms of a return on *costs of production* so that it can be applied, in the case of a risk contract, to the agreed estimated costs. Such a calculation is illustrated in Figure 9.1.

An Illustration

Step 1 – Choose the appropriate profit formula, in this example, the risk profit formula:

9.7% on capital employed + 4.6% on cost of production

Step 2 – Convert the 9.7% on CE portion to a percentage on CP by dividing the 9.7% by the CP:CE ratio, assumed to be 3 in this example:

9.7% on capital employed = (9.7 / 3)% on cost of production = 3.23% on cost of production

Step 3 – Add the two profit elements together, 3.23% on cost of production + 4.6% on cost of production giving 7.83% as the profit rate to be applied to this particular contractor's estimated cost of production.

Figure 9.1 Calculating the profit rate using the profit formula

The conversion from profit on capital employed to profit on costs of production is achieved by dividing the return on capital by the contractor's CP:CE ratio for the appropriate year. Capital employed (defined earlier) can be obtained from the company's Balance Sheet, costs of production from the company's Profit and Loss Account. Figure 9.1 assumes a contractor with a higher than average CP:CE ratio of 3:1. In this case, applying the risk profit formula produces a risk profit rate of 7.83 per cent on costs of production. Repeating the calculations for a contractor with a lower than average CP:CE ratio of 2:1 would give a higher risk rate of profit of 9.45 per cent on cost of production.

Contractors with higher than average CP:CE ratios typically have low levels of capital employed. The profit required from the capital based element of the profit formula is therefore lower than for a contractor with larger sums invested in capital employed (such as production equipment, stock, work in progress). Consultants would tend to have high CP:CE ratios while a heavy engineering company would probably have a low CP:CE ratio.

❏ The profit formula as a yardstick

For those who need to use the profit formula on a regular basis in contract pricing, the above explanation can only serve as an introduction. The number of such people is limited, though the annual level of expenditure involving profit formula contracts is currently about £2–3 billion. Specialist staff using the formula do have more detailed guidance manuals available to help them. The formula is of wider interest, however, as a yardstick for procurement staff involved only with contracts subject to competitive tendering.

Because of their exposure to competitive markets alone, many procurement staff may have little feel for the going rates of profit associated with their contractors and the types of purchases with which they are involved. On those occasions when a price break-down is required by the purchaser, the level of profit claimed is frequently unchallenged.

Instinctively, if pressed, many procurement staff, both in the public and private sectors, might consider a return of about 20 per cent on a contract to be reasonable. What is less certain is what that 20 per cent means. Is it a rate of return on capital employed or on costs of production? The difference is crucial as the profitability of a company which achieves a return on costs of production of 20 per cent is, on average, about twice that of a company which achieves a return on capital employed of 20 per cent .

As the earlier calculations illustrating the use of the profit formula in practice have shown, it was necessary to use the contractor's CP:CE ratio to convert a rate of return on capital employed to a rate of return on costs of production. Taking the 20 per cent guesstimate as a fair return on contractor's *capital employed* (coincidentally extremely close to the target rate of return of 19.45 per cent calculated by the Review Board for Government Contracts), this figure needs to be *divided* by the contractor's CP:CE ratio to give a rate of return which can be applied to the costs of production shown in a price breakdown. In the absence of more accurate information, using the average CP:CE ratio of 2.12:1 gives a return on costs of production of about 9.5 per cent.

This, then, is *a very rough guide* to the sort of profit rate which a purchaser should expect to see in a price breakdown, unless, of course, there were very specific reasons why it should be higher or lower. If a 20 per cent return on cost of production were being used by the contractor in a price breakdown, this would be equivalent to a return of over 40 per cent on capital employed for a contractor with an average CP:CE ratio!

❏ The price incentive

For any contract priced on the basis of the supplier's estimated costs, whether in a competitive or non-competitive market, the amount of profit included within the price is purely hypothetical at the outset of the contract. This is because that precise level of profit will only be achieved if the contractor's costs incurred in carrying out the work are precisely those originally estimated. If the contractor beats the cost estimate, a greater level of profit will be achieved; if the contract incurs costs which are greater than those estimated, a lower profit, or even a loss, will be the result.

Consider the following price breakdown as being the basis of a contract price:

	£
Labour hours	
400 @ £6.50 per hour	2600.00
Overheads @ 280%	7280.00
Raw material	1500.74
Subcontracts	2200.38
Bought-in finished parts	450.62
Total estimated costs	14031.74
Profit @ 9.2%	1290.92
Price each	15322.66

The attractiveness of such a price and pricing arrangement to a contractor is not just that a return of 9.2 per cent on costs of production may, in theory, be achieved, (which for a company with a CP:CE ratio of 2:1 will give a return on capital employed of a creditable 18.4 per cent), but that the cost estimate may be beaten by being more efficient and effective in carrying out the work. Taking the figures above, a 4 per cent reduction in labour hours and a saving of 5 per cent on the costs of raw materials, subcontracts and bought-in finished parts would increase profit to £1893.71, or 14.1 per cent of the costs.

For a company with a CP:CE ratio of 2:1, this would increase the return on capital employed to 28.2 per cent, a handsome return. A small change in costs has a large impact on rates of return, potentially either positive or negative, emphasising the incentive for the contractor to achieve high levels of efficiency.

Reference

Review Board for Government Contracts (1993) *Report of the Seventh General Review of the Profit Formula for Non-Competitive Government Contracts*London, HMSO March

Chapter 10

Purchase negotiation

In chapter 2, it was suggested that there were four main objectives in central Government procurement activity:

(i) to provide end users with what they need, when they need it, at the best value for money

(ii) to provide Accounting Officers, and through them Parliament and the taxpayer, with value for money through expenditure on procurement

(iii) to protect the Accounting Officer's interests in procurement, by means of appropriate managerial and contractual arrangements

(iv) to contribute to the corporate management of a department.

In trying to meet these objectives, the need to negotiate may arise at a number of points. People are well aware that buyers and suppliers will negotiate on price, terms and conditions. The purchaser may also end up negotiating with internal customers about some element of a specification or the use of a particular supplier. Furthermore, persuading senior managers that the purchasing function should be treated as an integral part of management may require some negotiating skills. This chapter, however, will concentrate on negotation between buyers and sellers.

Attitudes to negotiation

Many people do not like negotiating, whether it is a matter of persuading the garage to rectify a poor repair, of reaching agreement with the neighbours on their cats' access to their garden or of attempting to get a better deal when selling a used car. People find it embarrassing and either avoid doing it or do it without any real conviction, in case they lose their nerve and need an easy way out. They say things like,

I don't suppose you'll take any less,

without seriously expecting the seller to say,

of course, I'll let you have it for half the price!

The slightly braver buyer may say to the seller,

> I'd like to buy it but I really can't afford that price

If the price has been set *really* high, the seller may offer a reduction, out of sympathy – if the buyer takes two! Or the seller may show the buyer something a bit cheaper than is really wanted, leaving the buyer with the problem of how to steer the discussion back to the item which could not be afforded, without losing face. All very embarrassing!

In everyday life many people develop buying styles and attitudes to help them avoid the uncertainties and uncomfortable feelings that stem from attempts at negotiating. They say, or perhaps just think:

> it really isn't worth all the effort

or,

> they'll think I can't afford it

or, even worse,

> it must be good because look how much I've had to pay and how long I've had to wait for delivery.

Similar attitudes are occasionally met in procurement organisations, in both the private and public sector.

❏ Importance of self-belief

In the public sector, some believe, negotiation avoidance may stem from a perception that the seller is more skilled in negotiating, more knowledgeable of the requirement, has more power and authority, is more motivated, or is more professional than the buyer. Even if all this is totally untrue, the buyer's own belief will produce the same result as if it were true.

The purchasing power of the procurement organisation, particularly during the negotiation stages, stems from a belief in itself. Passive, mechanistic, unimaginative purchasing organisations frequently hide behind administrative procedures to avoid risk, rather than manage it, and use the procedures to justify their poor performance. The opportunities to negotiate a better deal will be actively sought by the best procurement organisations. They will not be put off by the fear of failure and a need to appease the supplier, as they will be knowledgeable, well-trained and confident.

❏ Win/win agreement?

Generally speaking, public servants are very reasonable people. They readily appreciate that they cannot have everything their own way in a negotiation and will have to concede something if agreement is to be reached. The idea of a win/win situation, where both parties stand to gain, has a great deal of natural appeal to them. It will encourage cooperation not confrontation, emphasising trust and interdependence. As an *outcome* of a negotiation, a win/win situation may be fine, but there can be dangers in setting that as the desired outcome at the beginning. It is certainly a risk to offer a win/win situation in the early stages of the negotiation.

There is a distinct danger that the seller will be able to take advantage of the buyer who is too reasonable, too soon. A reasonable approach may be good for a less-stressful life, but it does not necessarily serve for the tax payer. Just as a supplier's initial offer will be pitched at a level which will 'do them very nicely', particularly in a sole source situation, a buyer's counter-offer needs to be pitched to allow room for manoeuvre, so that when agreement is reached, a win/win outcome is more likely.

It needs to be remembered that win/win negotiations hardly ever mean 50/50 deals. In Government procurement negotiations, it is rare to find out what the other party truly achieved, except, perhaps, in the case of MOD post-costed contracts. Was the real outcome 70/30, 30/70 or 10/90? All that we should assume is that we could always have done at least a little better, with an outcome which, while still benefiting both parties, could have rewarded a more skilled buyer a little more.

It is not being suggested that purchase negotiations should be conducted in an atmosphere of mutual mistrust, with the other party being seen as the enemy. It is just that a firm self-belief, a belief in the organisation, a strong desire to achieve more, and maneuvering room in which to negotiate, are prerequisites of any successful purchase negotiation.

Basic principles of successful negotiation

In the remainder of this chapter, there are some introductory hints on successful negotiation. They are only an introduction and those seeking more guidance on this specific topic should consult one of the specialist texts. The topics briefly covered below are:

- recognition of negotiation power
- preparation and planning
- setting objectives

- effective ways to make concessions
- listening rules and techniques.

❑ Recognition of negotiating power

It can be only too easy for the public sector buyer, particularly the Government buyer, to underrate the need that the supplier has for the contract. Ask the question:

why do companies want to sell to Government?

What does a Government contract give them that other work does not? Here are five factors, each of which has a value to the supplier, and, if understood, confers power to the buyer:

- the potential business is huge, and there is enormous scope for any company which can become a regular supplier across a range of departments
- Government departments are the quickest payers around, and payment is certain
- 'cold-selling' to find new customers in the private sector is very costly, and the number of takers is few
- a Government contract can give security and a better image
- individual Government contracts tend to be larger than those in the private sector.

There are other power factors at play in a purchase negotiation, such as:

- the power of the purchasing organisation, as perceived by the seller
- the power which comes from personal commitment by the purchaser
- the power of time and patience, when the procurement has been properly planned and the purchaser is not faced with unrealistic deadlines.

These powers can all be positively used by the Government purchaser to achieve a successful conclusion to a negotiation. However, the power first needs to be recognised.

The party who holds the power in a negotiation is the one who *believes* they have it, and who is *allowed* by the other party to believe it, irrespective of who really has the power. This is one of the reasons why the outcome of most negotiations is so heavily dependent on individual negotiators and their skills and their attitudes, rather than on facts alone. It is also why the returns from investment in effective negotiation training and opportunities for self-development are so great.

Relatively small changes in negotiators' skill and attitude can lead to large improvements in the results of their negotiations.

❑ Preparation and planning

Successful purchase negotiations stem from thorough planning and preparation. It is often said that, for every hour spent in successful face-to-face negotiations, a further ten to fifteen will have been spent in preparation. This will depend, of course, on the nature of the negotiation, but the great danger of too little preparation is that it is nearly impossible to rectify, without at least some loss, once the negotiation is under way.

Critical areas of preparation are:

- knowledge of the product or service being purchased
  - general understanding of what is being purchased
  - the intended use
  - possible alternatives
  - future requirements
- knowledge of the seller's strengths
  - how much the seller wants the contract
  - how confident the seller is of getting it
  - how much time is available to the seller to reach agreement
- knowledge of the buyer's strengths
  - the buyer's negotiating power
  - the amount of competition in the market
- knowledge of the seller
  - the company and its representatives
- knowledge of cost or price analysis (where appropriate)
  - information provided by cost estimators and accountants.

In relation to the first category, knowledge of the product or service, it is important to emphasise that the buyer does *not* need an understanding of all the technical details. The prime requirement is knowledge of what the item is intended to do and how it will have to perform.

❑ Setting objectives

Specific negotiation objectives need to be established once the preparation phase has been 'completed'. For each variable on which it is planned to negotiate, an objective is required in the form of a specific target, a minimum and a maximum. However, some care is necessary. There is a danger that these objectives will unduly constrain the approach, such that relevant information extracted from the supplier is ignored if it doesn't fit the objectives, rather than being allowed to modify the objectives to reflect the data obtained. Some individuals find it easier to be flexible and to keep their options open than others. Flexibility is one of the hallmarks of a good negotiator, but flexibility based on a reading of the evidence, not flexibility which is simply compliance.

❑ Effective ways to make concessions

Knowing how to gain movement and make movement are essential to successful negotiating, yet the author's personal experience in providing training in negotiation over many years is that this knowledge, if known, is rarely applied. Frequently the parties to a negotiation *want* to move towards each other, but don't know *how* to without losing face. Stalemate and bitterness result, as neither side knows how to make it easier for the other party to move.

Learning how to concede may appear to be an odd route to more successful negotiations, but achieving movement in a negotiation is vital if stalemate is to be avoided. Most of this is common sense. When thinking objectively and unemotionally, we realise that, when making concessions, we should not:

- concede too much at a time, because few people appreciate anything which they get too easily, and it could lead the other party to expect more
- concede too soon, especially on a major issue, because it may look submissive and the other party will expect more
- concede anything without getting something in return
- concede anything without knowing its value to *both* parties
- concede at any price, just to get a deal; it may be necessary to say 'no'.

Putting these in a more positive way and adding a few more common sense thoughts, gives the following *Ten Concession Guidelines*.

1 Time concessions carefully – move *slowly*.

2 Make *small* concessions.

3 Make the other party appreciate and value the concession by making them work for it.

4 *Trade* each concession; get something in return.

5 Treat every concession as money in absolute terms, not as a percentage of the total contract: a series of small concessions rapidly adds up.

6 Make room for concessions to be made; as a buyer, start low, but be prepared to justify the starting point.

7 Put a value on the concession *before* it is made, not once it has been accepted.

8 Value the concession in the other party's terms as well as your own.

9 Trade concessions that are cheap for you to give, but are worth a lot to the other party.

10 Say 'no deal' if you have to.

These 'guidelines', like much advice on negotiating, are, as said earlier basically common sense, but unfortunately this is often the first sense to be lost during a demanding negotiation! (The second to be lost in a negotiation is usually our hearing!) In one's first experiences of negotiation it is vital to think hard all the time about the approach to concessions; the approach needs to become second nature.

❑ Listening rules and techniques

The ability to achieve movement in a negotiation is of little value if the concession goes unheard! The ability to listen effectively can be an extremely difficult skill to learn, perhaps because we live in a society where talking is often associated with power and listening with weakness, or because we may work in an environment where the same is true.

Talking too much in a negotiation can be dangerous by:

- giving information, perhaps more than was intended, but not only talking too much but also saying too much
- losing the opportunity to receive information from the other party
- giving the other party time to think
- putting enormous pressure on the talker and taking the pressure off the other party.

115

Learning to listen is hard, but with some rules to follow and some techniques to practice it can be made a little easier. Once again, the advice is little more than common sense, but because of that, one should take it and practice it when able, outside the negotiation, until it is second nature.

Some listening rules and techniques are as follows:

- as far as possible, plan important questions in advance, so as to be able to listen to the answer carefully without having to think of the next question
- stay silent and keep listening until the other party has finished answering a question or explaining a point
- do not mentally phrase clever responses while the other person is still answering or explaining
- listen to understand what is being said, not to beat the other party in an argument
- show the other party that you *are* listening
- listen patiently
- if subject to a tendency to interrupt, listen with the head slightly tilted to one side, as this makes it difficult to speak
- check your listening and understanding by regularly summing up, especially as the overall package takes shape.

In the area of listening, as in those other areas where everything seems to be common sense, training tends to be important. This is because it gives people an opportunity to stand back and review their own performance and approach objectively with advice from experienced observers.

❏ Background knowledge

Negotiating is not a skill which can be developed in isolation. Successful negotiators have a broad experience of business matters and management tools such as accounting, economics, contract law and quantitative analysis. They are knowledgeable about the products and services they buy. Along with these attributes, the best purchase negotiators are those who *want more* from each negotiation than do their counterparts; as in most things motivation and attitude are critical success factors.

References

Kennedy, G (1991) *Everything is Negotiable* London, Arrow Books

Kennedy, G (1987) *Pocket Negotiator* Oxford, Basil Blackwell and The Economist Publications

Lidstone, J (1977) *Negotiating Profitable Sales* Aldershot, Gower Press

Sheridan, D (1990) *Negotiating Commercial Contracts* Maidenhead, McGraw Hill

Chapter 11

The European Community

Supplies and Services Directives

EC directives, issued by the EC Council of Ministers, are binding on EC member states. Each member state is required to implement the directives through national legislation within the time period allowed by the directives.

The EC *Supplies* Directives, 77/62/EEC, 80/767/EEC and 88/295/EEC were implemented in UK law by the Public Supply Contracts Regulations which came into force in December 1991. These directives were subsequently amalgamated into the consolidated Supplies Directive, 93/36/EEC, in June 1993 and further secondary legislation will bring this consolidated directive into UK law.

The EC *Services* Directive, 92/50/EEC, was implemented by the Public Services Contracts Regulations which came into force in January 1994. Separate directives exist to cover the public procurement of works projects and utilities, and although similar principles apply, these are not considered in this book.

The impact of the European Community's Supplies Directive and Services Directive has been widespread across Government. Heads of procurement organisations have been given the added responsibility of ensuring compliance with the directives throughout the organisation, a task which has been particularly difficult in those departments where the purchase of goods and services has been fragmented.

In those areas where a planned and systematic approach to procurement does not yet exist, there is a danger that the directives are seen as a burden rather than as a means of achieving better overall value for money. The purchasing organisations which appear to face the most resistance when applying the directives within their organisation are those which are not involved in the procurement process as a whole, that are not pro-active and who are perceived only as administrative agents. The directives, which are administered by the European Commission, principally aim to:

- increase the transparency of procurement procedures and practice throughout the Community
- aid the free movement of goods and services between member states

- develop the conditions of effective competition for public supply and service contracts.

They do this by:

- setting down thresholds above which the directives apply
- defining certain minimum time limits for advance information notices, for the tender period and for the contract award notice
- defining the extent of any exemptions by sector
- limiting the use of single tender action
- defining the circumstances where extreme urgency can be invoked
- adopting common rules in respect of standardisation in the technical field.

The key areas of the directives and Public Contracts Regulations which are covered in this chapter are:

- pre-tender publicity and information
- tendering procedure
- supplier appraisal
- technical standards and specifications
- sub-division of contracts.

Pre-tender publicity and information

Under the terms of the directives and the Public Contracts Regulations, each contracting authority in Government (effectively, each department) must give potential suppliers advance information on public procurement programmes. This is done through an 'Annual Notice' for supplies or a 'Prior Information Notice' for services (both often known as 'indicative notices' or referred to as the 'pre-information procedures').

❑ Annual notices/prior information notices

A pre-information procedure has to be followed in respect of both supply and service needs. This procedure requires that:

- as soon as possible after commencement of the financial year
- an Annual Notice or Prior Information Notice as appropriate is placed in the *Supplement of the Official Journal of the European Communities (OJEC)*
- setting out by product (for the Supplies Directive) or by service (for the Service Directive)

- the total estimated contract value of the requirements for the coming twelve months
- where these requirements equal or exceed a threshold, currently £561,480 excluding VAT (or 750,000 ECUs).

In calculating the total value of the supplies or service requirements, to determine whether or not a Notice is required, only those anticipated contracts subject to one of the advertising procedures described later in this chapter, need be included. This excludes from the total those contracts which will *not* need to be advertised under one of the procurement procedures, either because they fall below the individual threshold, or because they are exempt in some other way.

For example, assume that a contracting authority anticipates the five contracts shown in Figure 11.1. In this case, the maintenance and repair of vehicles and equipment would be excluded as it is below the current individual service threshold of £149,728 excluding VAT (200,000 ECUs). The meal serving services with full restaurant service would be excluded because it is exempt from the full Regulations (Schedule 1, Part B of the Services Regulations refers). Together, the remaining three exceed the Notice threshold of £561,480 and therefore such a notice is required.

Anticipated Contracts		
Requirement	**Estimated Value**	**Included**
Building cleaning services	£190,000	Yes
Programming services	£193,000	Yes
Maintenance and repair of vehicles and equipment	£110,000	No
Management consultancy services	£180,000	Yes
Meal serving services with full restaurant service	£210,000	No
Total Estimated Value of Contracts Included	**£563,000**	

Figure 11.1 Determining the need for an Indicative Notice for a service requirement

A similar approach is adopted for the Annual Notice required under the Public Supply Contracts Regulations, except that the individual threshold is currently £96,403 excluding VAT (130,000 Special Drawing Rights). This is the threshold for General Agreement on Tariffs and Trade (GATT) Contracting Authorities, these being mainly central Government departments and listed in Schedule 1 of the Public Supply Contract Regulations. A higher threshold of £149,728 excluding VAT (200,000 ECUs) would apply to other contracting authorities such as local government and also to certain requirements of the Ministry of Defence.

An Annual or Prior Information Notice would contain the information shown in Figure 11.2. This Notice gives the market advance information of requirements, to enable potential suppliers to plan ahead and to allow every opportunity for effective competition across the Community when the requirement is eventually advertised under one of the procurement procedures described later in this chapter.

Pre-information procedures

1 **Awarding authority:** Name, address and telephone, telegraphic, telex and facsimile numbers of the awarding authority.

2 **Nature and quantity or value:** Identification of the products or services to be supplied.

3 **Award procedure expected to commence on:** Estimated date of commencement of the procedures of the award of contract(s) (if known).

4 **Other information:** eg relevant telephone contact numbers, etc.

5 **Notice postmarked:** Date of despatch of the Notice.

6 **Notice received:** Date of receipt of the Notice by the Office for Official Publications of the European Communities.

Figure 11.2 Annual or Prior Information Notice

❏ Aggregation

Difficulties may be experienced in estimating the value of a requirement for the purposes of the Procurement Directives, particularly if the contracting authority seeks to enter into a series of contracts or there is a recurrent need for the requirement. In these cases, Article 5 of the Supplies Directive and Article 7 of the Services Directive apply.

If a contracting authority seeks to enter into two or more contracts at the same time for goods of a particular type, then the estimated value of the total sum of these requirements is used for threshold purposes. Where the total sum is equal to or greater than the £96,403, then the Directive applies to all of the proposed contracts.

If a service requirement is subdivided into several lots, each one the subject of a contract, and the total estimated value of the purchases is greater than £149,728, then the provisions of the Service Directive shall apply to all of the individual purchases. The exception is that contracting authorities may waive the application of the Directive for any purchase which has an estimated value of less than £59,891 (80,000 ECUs), provided that the total value of such 'low value' purchases does not exceed 20 per cent of the total estimated value of the whole package.

Where a proposed contract provides for options, the basis of calculating the contract value shall include the value of the options.

Where a requirement is for both services and supplies, it falls within the provisions of the Services Directive when the value of the service element exceeds that of the supplies element.

❑ Recurrent needs

Where there is a recurrent need for goods or services, and the contracting authority enters into:

- a series of contracts at different times
- a contract which is renewable
- a contract for an indefinite period

there are two methods of valuing the requirement for threshold purposes:

- to take the previous twelve months' aggregated total payments for goods or services of that type and adjust it for anticipated changes for the next twelve months
- to estimate the value of the next twelve months' aggregated requirement for goods or services of that type, starting from the first delivery, or for the duration of the contract where this is greater than twelve months.

However, where goods or services are to be used solely by a discrete operational unit within the contracting authority, with sole control over purchasing these goods or services, then the valuation for threshold purposes shall be in respect of the goods or services required by that unit alone.

❑ Advertising in the *Official Journal of the European Communities* – Contract Notices

If the estimated value of a contract requirement is, currently, equal to or greater than £96,403 (for supplies required by GATT contracting authorities), or equal to or greater than £149,728 (for services), then the anticipated contract is required to be advertised by the contracting authority as a Contract Notice in the OJEC Supplement. This applies whether or not the supplies are purchased outright, leased, rented or subject to a hire purchase agreement. To ensure impartiality, the potential contract requirement must not be advertised in the UK before the Tender Notice is sent for publication in the OJEC Supplement for all to see. Furthermore, should a national advert be used at an appropriate time, it must not contain any information other than that published in the *Official Journal*. As well as appearing in the *OJEC Supplement*, the notices are accessed by subscribers to the Tenders Electronic Daily (TED) database.

The date of despatch of the notice by the contracting authority is a crucial reference point, because some of the minimum time limits allowed under the Regulations start from this date. The date of despatch means the date on which the notice is actually sent to the Official Publications Office, and not the date shown on the documents sent for publication, which could naturally be much earlier.

❑ Evaluation criteria

The contract award criteria must be included in the Contract Notice and only the criteria specified in the Notice may be used at the tender evaluation stage. Both the Supplies and Services Directives require that the criteria shall be either:

- the lowest price only, or
- the most economically advantageous tender.

As it is Government procurement policy to seek the best *overall* value for money, which cannot be judged on price alone, the Contract Notices list the tender evaluation criteria to be applied, in descending order of importance where practicable, for example, quality, price, delivery, and so on.

Tendering procedures

The Supplies and Services Directives, and the corresponding Public Supply and Services Regulations, permit the use of three forms of tendering procedure. These are known as:

- the Open Procedure
- the Restricted Procedure
- the Negotiated Procedure.

❏ The Open Procedure

Under the Open Procedure, the Contract Notice advertising the requirement is despatched by the procurement organisation and published in the *OJEC Supplement*. Thereafter, *all* interested suppliers who respond to the advertisement are invited to tender for the requirement. The Open Procedure is generally used where the procurement organisation anticipate that competition is likely to be very limited because of the few, known, available suppliers. The use of the Open Procedure increases the level of interest and competition to the maximum available, since all interested suppliers are invited to tender. However, the nature and value of the requirement needs to be such as to justify committing the large level of resources which could well be needed to manage effectively a potentially large volume of tenders.

A Contract Notice for Supplies under the Open Procedure would contain the information shown in Annex B, Item 1, while a Contract Notice for a Service would contain the information shown in Annex B, Item 2.

Before describing the Open Procedure in more detail, Figure 11.3 gives an outline of the process and the timescales required. It can be seen from Figure 11.3 that a prescribed minimum period of 52 days must be set aside from the date of despatch of the Contract Notice to allow the tenderers to return the completed tender documents. This time limit is reduced to 36 days if an Annual or Prior Information Notice has been published under the Pre-Information Procedures described earlier in this chapter.

Figure 11.3 also shows that invitation to tender documents are sent to all suppliers who respond to the Notice by the date specified. These documents must be sent within six days of receiving the request to participate. When requested by the tenderers, additional information relating to the tender documents must be supplied by the purchasing organisation not less than six days before the deadline for receipt of the tenders. On some occasions, particularly in the case of the procurement of services, tenderers may require a site visit in order to complete their tender. When this is so, the period for receipt of tenders must be extended by a reasonable length.

The Supplies and Services Directives do not set a specific timescale for the supplier appraisal phase of the procurement because, under the Open Procedure, the number of tenderers is unknown at the outset. Therefore, the procurement organisation needs to plan sufficient resources, in terms of both time and effort, for this potentially time consuming activity. In practice, as the Open Procedure is normally chosen where the number of potential suppliers is believed to be relatively few, the appraisal process should never be too onerous. However, if this procedure has been used to 'explore' the market potential, the number of responses could be very high, and the corresponding burden of supplier appraisal severe.

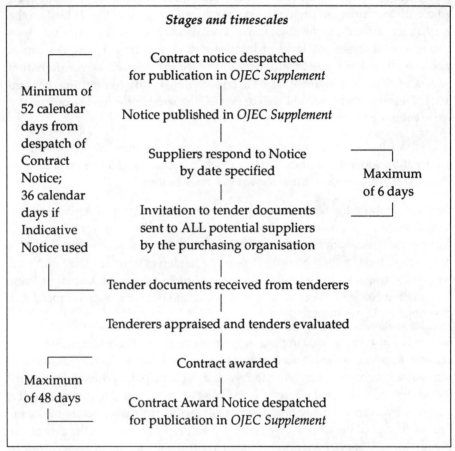

Figure 11.3 Open Procedure for the procurement of supplies and services

❑ The Restricted Procedure

Under the Restricted Procedure, a Contract Notice advertising the requirement is despatched and published in the *OJEC Supplement*. Suppliers then notify the contracting authority of their interest. Under the Open Procedure *all* of these would be invited to tender. However, under the Restricted Procedure, the contracting authority will select, from among the interested parties, those who may submit tenders. This is the procedure most commonly used by UK government departments for supplies requirements. Until recently, special justification was required for the use of the Restricted Procedure for the purchase of supplies, but the Consolidated Supplies Directive has placed the Open and Restricted Procedures on the same footing, in line with the Services Directive. Under the Services Directive, the Restricted Procedure may be freely chosen in preference to the Open Procedure if it seems more appropriate in a particular case.

A Contract Notice for supplies to be procured under the Restricted Procedure would contain the information shown in Annex B, Item 3. The content has much in common with that for the Open Procedure shown in Annex B, Item 1 but it reflects the fact that those responding are applying at this stage only to be included among those invited to tender. The same point applies in the case of services. A Contract Notice for a service requirement to be procured under the Restricted Procedure would contain the information shown in Annex B, Item 4.

Before the Restricted Procedure is described in more detail, Figure 11.4 gives an outline of the process and the timescales required. It can be seen from Figure 11.4 that, under the normal Restricted Procedure, a prescribed minimum period of 37 days is set aside from the date of despatch of the Contract Notice to give interested suppliers sufficient time to respond. This period may be reduced to 26 calendar days in those cases where an Annual or Prior Information Notice under the pre-information procedure has been used.

The information provided by the suppliers in response to the 'qualifications' section of the Contract Notice allows a supplier appraisal exercise to be conducted by the procurement organisation, so that only those suppliers who satisfy the department's supplier appraisal criteria are subsequently invited to tender.

Under the Restricted Procedure, using the 'normal' timescales, tenderers are given a minimum of 40 calendar days from the date of despatch of the tender documents in which to complete and return their tender. When requested by the tenderers, additional information relating to the tender documents must be supplied by the purchasing organisation not less than six calendar days before the deadline for receipt of the tenders. On some occasions, particularly in the case of the procurement of services, tenderers may require a site visit in order to complete their tender. When this is so, the period for receipt of tenders must be extended by a reasonable length.

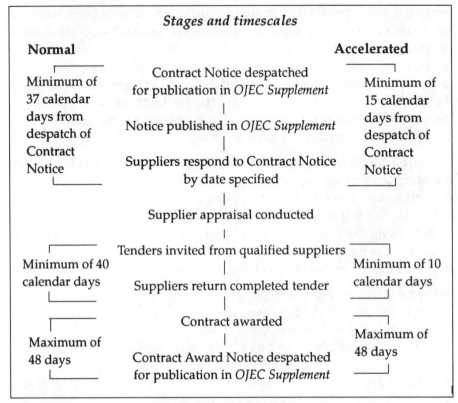

Stages and timescales

Normal		**Accelerated**
Minimum of 37 calendar days from despatch of Contract Notice	Contract Notice despatched for publication in *OJEC Supplement* Notice published in *OJEC Supplement* Suppliers respond to Contract Notice by date specified	Minimum of 15 calendar days from despatch of Contract Notice
	Supplier appraisal conducted	
Minimum of 40 calendar days	Tenders invited from qualified suppliers Suppliers return completed tender	Minimum of 10 calendar days
Maximum of 48 days	Contract awarded Contract Award Notice despatched for publication in *OJEC Supplement*	Maximum of 48 days

Figure 11.4 Restricted Procedure for the procurement of supplies and services

❏ Accelerated Restricted Procedure

When using the Restricted Procedure, the 'normal' timescale may be shortened by using the accelerated procedure, but only when operational urgency makes impracticable any of the normal minimum time limits. It must not be used simply as a means of avoiding the normal time limits. As shown in Figure 11.4, the period from the date of despatch of the Notice to the date by which requests from suppliers to participate must be received shall not be less than fifteen calendar days. In addition, the period for receipt of completed tenders must not be less than ten calendar days from the date of despatch of the invitation to tender. When requested by the tenderers, additional information relating to the tender documents must be supplied by the purchasing organisation not less than four calendar days before the deadline for receipt of the tenders.

The justification for the use of the accelerated procedure must be stated by the purchasing organisation in the Notice published in the *OJEC Supplement*, at paragraph 2(b) of the Notice in respect of supplies and at paragraph 10(a) of the Notice in respect of services.

The Negotiated Procedure

The Negotiated Procedure is a procedure whereby a contract may be awarded by the contracting authority after negotiation of the contract terms with one or more selected suppliers. Under the EC Procurement Directives and the Public Contracts Regulations, this procedure is permitted in certain circumstances. For *Supplies*, the six criteria under which the Negotiated Procedure is permitted are:

- when no valid or acceptable tenders have been received in response to a Contract Notice under the Open or Restricted Procedures

- when *no* tenders have been received in reponse to a Contract Notice under the Open or Restricted Procedures and the requirement is substantially unchanged – provided that a report is initiated for the Treasury for onward transmission to the Commission

- when the requirement is for research, experiment, study or development

- when the goods may only be provided by a particular supplier for technical, artistic or intellectual property right reasons

- when the requirement is unforeseeable by and not attributable to the contracting authority and the time limits prescribed under the Open and Restricted Procedures cannot be met

- when for reasons of compatibility or disproportionate technical difficulties in operation and maintenance an additional requirement needs to be met by the original supplier (generally, for no longer than three years).

For *Services*, the eight criteria under which the Negotiated Procedure is permitted are:

- when no valid or acceptable tenders have been received in response to a Contract Notice under the Open or Restricted Procedures

- when no tenders have been received in reponse to a Contract Notice under the Open or Restricted Procedures and the requirement is substantially unchanged

- when the nature of the service to be provided or the associated risks do not permit prior overall pricing

- where the nature of the services provided is such that an adequate specification cannot be drawn up to permit the Open or Restricted procedure to be used

- when the service may only be provided by a particular supplier for technical, artistic or intellectual property right reasons

- when the rules of a Design Contest require the contract to be awarded to the successful contestant(s), provided that all successful contestants are invited to negotiate the contract

- when the requirement is unforeseeable by and not attributatble to the contracting authority and the time limits prescribed under the Open and Restricted Procedures cannot be met

- when additional services are required which were not included in the original project through unforeseeable circumstances and which cannot be provided separately for technical or economic reasons and are strictly necessary – though not exceeding 50 per cent of the original contract value.

The use of this procedure may first need to be advertised in the *OJEC Supplement* with a 'Negotiated Procedures' Notice as described below.

❑ Negotiated Procedure *with* prior publication of a Contract Notice

If the intention is *not* to include in the negotiations all of the suppliers who submitted tenders under the original procurement procedure, then it is necessary to publish a Negotiated Procedure Notice in the *OJEC Supplement*. The information contained in such a Notice for Supplies and Services is shown at Annex B, Items 5 and 6 respectively. The prescribed timescales and procedure are outlined in Figure 11.5.

❑ Negotiated procedure *without* prior publication of a Contract Notice

The Negotiated Procedure may be used without prior publication of a Negotiated Procedures Notice as long as:

- each previous tenderer under the unsuccessful Open or Restricted Procedure is invited to negotiate the contract
- the requirement is substantially unchanged

and, in the case of a service requirement, the reason for using the Negotiated Procedure is neither:

- the inability to achieve prior overall pricing, nor
- the inability to draw up an adequate specification.

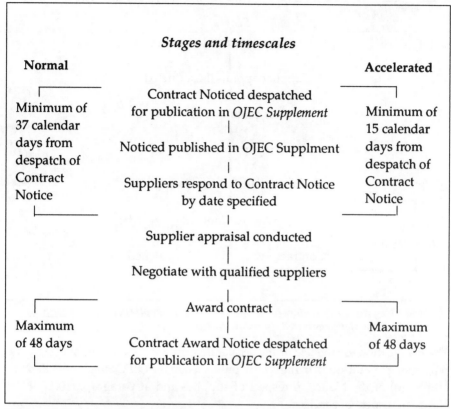

Stages and timescales

| Normal | | Accelerated |

┌──────── Contract Noticed despatched ┌────────
Minimum of   for publication in *OJEC Supplement*   Minimum of
37 calendar | 15 calendar
days from   Noticed published in OJEC Supplment   days from
despatch of | despatch of
Contract   Suppliers respond to Contract Notice   Contract
Notice   by date specified   Notice
└──────── | └────────

Supplier appraisal conducted
|
Negotiate with qualified suppliers
|
┌──────── Award contract ┌────────
Maximum | Maximum
of 48 days   Contract Award Notice despatched   of 48 days
└────────   for publication in *OJEC Supplement*   └────────

Figure 11.5 Negotiated Procedure for the procurement of supplies or services __with__ prior publication of a Negotiated Procedure Notice

When the Negotiated Procedure without prior publication of a Notice is employed as the method of procurement for either supplies or services, a written report is compiled by the procurement organisation to explain which of the permitted circumstances constituted the grounds for using that procedure. The main elements of this procurement procedure are outlined in Figure 11.6.

❏ Accelerated Negotiated Procedure

Under the EC Procurement Directives, it is permitted to use an accelerated Negotiated Procedure but only with prior publication of a Contract Notice. As shown in Figure 11.5, the period from the date of despatch of the Accelerated Negotiated Procedure Notice to the deadline for receipt of requests to participate must not be less than fifteen calendar days.

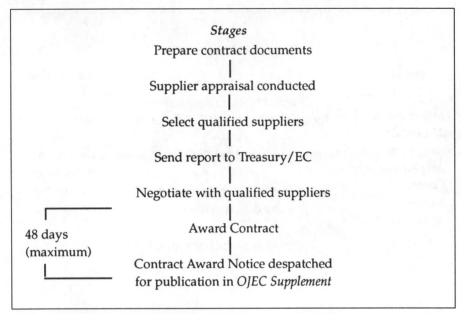

Figure 11.6 Negotiated Procedure for the procurement of supplies or services <u>without</u> prior publication of a Negotiated Procedure Notice

The justification for the use of the accelerated procedure must be stated by the purchasing organisation in the Notice published in the *OJEC Supplement*, at paragraph 2(b) of the Notice in respect of supplies and at paragraph 10(a) of the Notice in respect of services.

Supplier appraisal

The supplier appraisal conducted when using one of the procedures prescribed under the EC Procurement Directives follows the same general methodology as that of a domestic competitive tender process (see chapter 4). Typically, the financial information requested would comprise:

- a copy of, or extracts from, the supplier's balance sheets, where publication of the balance sheet is required under company law in the country in which the supplier is established
- appropriate statements from bankers
- a statement of the supplier's overall turnover, and its turnover in respect of the goods or services to which the requirement relates, for the previous three financial years.

Depending upon the nature, quantity and purpose of the goods to be supplied or service to be provided, the commercial and technical information requested as evidence of the supplier's capability might include:

- in the case of a service provider, the educational and professional qualifications of the supplier's managerial staff and those responsible for providing the service
- a list of the principal deliveries effected or services provided in the past three years, with the amounts, dates and recipients, public or private, involved
- a description of the supplier's technical facilities, their measures for ensuring quality and their study and research facilities
- an indication of the technicians or technical bodies involved, whether or not belonging directly to the supplier, especially those responsible for quality control
- samples, descriptions and photographs of the product to be supplied
- a statement of the service provider's average annual manpower and the number of managerial staff for the last three years
- a statement of the tool, plant or technical equipment available to the service provider for carrying out the service
- certificates drawn up by official quality control institutes or agencies of recognised competence, attesting conformity to certain specifications or standards of goods, clearly identified by references to specifications or standards
- an indication of the proportion of the contract which the service provider may intend to sub-contract.

Many Government departments maintain lists of appraised suppliers and these are sometimes used to expand the competitive field for a particular requirement by sending a selection of those suppliers a copy of the relevant Notice after it has been despatched for publication in the *OJEC*. Suppliers responding to the Notice who meet the minimum supplier appraisal standards are considered equally with those selected from the list of appraised suppliers.

❏ Contract Award Notices

It is a requirement of the EC Supplies and Services Directives that a Contract Award Notice be published no later than 48 days after the date of the contract. This applies whichever procurement procedure has been followed. The details to be published in the *OJEC Supplement* include

- the contract award criteria
- the name and address of the selected supplier

- the nature of the goods or services
- the contract price or range of prices tendered.

Futhermore, a Contract Award Notice is required for any contracts falling within the provisions of the Directives and the Public Contracts Regulations even if it was not originally advertised in the *Official Journal*.

The full details contained in the Contract Award Notice in respect of a requirement for supplies are shown in Figure 11.7.

---

1 **Awarding authority:** Name, address and telephone, telegraphic, telex and facsimile numbers of the contracting authority.

2 a) **Award procedure:** eg Negotiated procedure.

b) **Justification (Art. 6 (2,3)):** In respect of contracting authorities listed in Annex 1 to Directive 93/36/EEC, where appropriate, justification in accordance with Article 6(2) and 6(3) for the use of negotiated procedures eg 'for technical or artistic reasons or to protect exclusive rights'.

3 **Date of award:** Date of award of contract.

4 **Award criteria:** eg 'best value for money having regard to price, delivery and technical performance'.

5 **Tenders received:** Number of offers received.

6 **Supplier(s):** Name(s) and address(es) of supplier(s).

7 **Goods supplied:** Nature and quantity of goods supplied, by supplier, where applicable.

8 **Price(s):** Price or range of prices.

9 **Other information:**

10 **Notice published on:** Date of publication of the tender notice in the *Official Journal of the European Communities.*

11 **This notice postmarked:** Date of despatch of the Notice.

12 **This notice received on:** Date of receipt of the Notice by the Office for Official Publications of the European Communities.

Figure 11.7 Contract Award Notice – supplies

The details contained in the Contract Award Notice in respect of the procurement of a service are shown in Figure 11.8.

---

1 **Awarding authority:** Name, address and telephone, telegraphic, telex and facsimile numbers of the contracting authority.

2 **Award procedure chosen, justification (Article 11 (3)):** eg Restricted Procedure.

3 **Category of service and description, CPC reference number:** eg Category 27; CPC reference 84; computer and related services.

4 **Date of award of the contract:**

5 **Criteria:** eg 'best value for money having regard to price, delivery and quality'.

6 **Tenders received:** Number of offers received.

7 **Service provider(s):** Name and address of service provider(s).

8 **Price(s):** Price or range of prices.

9 **Subcontracts:** Where appropriate, the value and proportion of the contract which may be subcontracted to third parties.

10 **Other information:**

11 **Notice published on:** Date of publication of the tender notice in the *Official Journal of the European Communities*.

12 **Notice postmarked:** Date of despatch of the Notice.

13 **Notice received on:** Date of receipt of the Notice by the Office for Official Publications of the European Communities.

14 **Article 16(3):** For Residual Services, agreement by the contracting authority to publication of the Notice.

Figure 11.8 Contract Award Notice – services

Where release of certain information under a Contract Award Notice would either:

- impede law enforcement or otherwise be contrary to the public interest, or
- prejudice the legitimate commercial interests of potential enterprises, public or private, or

- prejudice competition between suppliers,

then this need not be published (Article 9.3 of Directive 93/36 and Article 16.5 of Directive 92/50 refer). For example, on some occasions, it may not be appropriate to publish the price or even a range of prices. If a tenderer believes that, for commercial reasons, information provided should not be published in a Contract Award Notice, this should be drawn to the attention of the contracting authority, together with reasons at the time of submitting their tender. The contracting authority can then consider the case on its merits against the above criteria.

Technical standards and specifications

It is usual to include in the tender documents not only the terms and conditions which will apply to any resulting contract, but also specification details such as the standards of quality, performance and safety required. In this respect, it is the responsibility of the purchasing organisation to ensure compliance with the requirements of the EC Procurement Directives upon the use of European Standards and common technical specifications.

A European Standard is a standard approved by the European Committee for Standardisation (CEN) or by the European Committee for Electrotechnical Standardisation (CENELEC). A common technical specification is a technical specification laid down in accordance with the procedure recognised by Member States with a view to uniform application across the Community. The Supplies and Service Directives, Articles 8.2 and 14.2 respectively, require UK contracting authorities to use either a British Standard implementing a European Standard wherever such a standard exists, or common technical specifications.

Article 8(2) of the Supplies Directive and Article 14(2) of the Services Directive state that:

> Without prejudice to the legally binding national technical rules and in so far as these are compatible with Community law, ... technical specifications ..... shall be defined by the contracting authorities by reference to national standards implementing European standards or by reference to European technical approvals or by reference to common technical specifications.

There are exceptions to this rule, and these are contained in Article 8(3) of the Supplies Directive and Article 14(3) of the Services Directive. The former, which is essentially the same as Article 14(3), is summarised as follows.

A contracting authority may depart from paragraph 2 if:

(a) the standards, European technical approvals or common technical specifications do not include any provision for establishing conformity, or, technical means do not exist for establishing satisfactorily the conformity of a product to these standards, European technical approvals or common technical specifications

(b) the application of paragraph 2 would prejudice the application of Council Directives on type approval, decisions on IT and telecomms standardisation or other Community instruments in specific service or product areas

(c) use of these standards, European technical approvals or common technical specifications would oblige the contracting authority to acquire supplies incompatible with equipment already in use or would entail disproportionate costs or technical difficulties, but only as a part of a clearly defined and recorded strategy with a view to change-over, within a given period, to European standards, European technical approvals or common technical specifications

(d) the project concerned is of a genuinely innovative nature for which the use of existing European standards, European technical approvals or common technical specifications would not be appropriate.

Justification of a derogation from Articles 8(2) and 14(2) of the Directives must be included in the Contract Notice published in the Supplement to the Official Journal of the European Communities, for example, see paragraph 3(d) of the Contract Notice for the procurement of supplies under the Open Procedure, shown at Annex B, Item 1. In addition, as the Member States or the Commission are entitled to see the reasons for the derogation, the justification must be kept on file.

If there is neither a British standard implementing a European standard nor a common technical specification or in the case where an exception applies, another standard may be used as long as it does not prejudice the principles of equivalence and mutual recognition of technical specifications. In these circumstances, the order of preference to be applied, contained in Article 8(5) of the Supplies Directive and Article 14(5) of the Services Directive, is as follows:

(i) British standards implementing international standards accepted in the UK

    (ii) other British standards

    (iii) any other standard.

The procurement of proprietary goods or services by way of a domestic UK purchase invariably involves a risk to value for money, as the level of competition has effectively been limited. The purchase of suitable equivalent alternatives, where possible, helps to avoid the difficulties associated with very narrow supply markets. As far as EC purchases are concerned, a firm stance is taken by the Directives to prohibit, wherever possible, the market distortions created by trade marks, patents and other specific sources of supply. Article 8(6) of the Supplies Directive and Article 14(6) of the Services Directive may be summarised as follows:

> Unless it is justified by the subject of the contract, Member States shall prohibit the introduction into the contract, of specifications which mention products of a specific make or source or of a particular process which favour or eliminate certain products or service providers. In particular, the indication of trade marks, patents, types of specific origin or production shall be prohibited. However, if such indication is accompanied by the words 'or equivalent', it shall be authorised in cases where the contracting authority is unable to give a description of the subject of the contract using specifications which are sufficiently precise and intelligible to all parties concerned.

❏ Call-off contracts

A 'call-off contract' is an arrangement whereby a purchaser enters into a contract for a *definite* quantity of a good to be delivered or amount of a service to be provided over an agreed period of time, at an agreed price or pricing arrangement. Under such an arrangement, the parties to the contract are legally bound to meet their contract obligations, the seller to deliver the specified goods in the amount, time and place requested in accordance with the terms of the contract, and the buyer must take delivery and pay the price in the amount and at the time agreed.

If the expected total value of such a call-off contract exceeds the appropriate supplies or service threshold, irrespective of the value of individual consignments, then it should be advertised in the OJEC Supplement.

❏ Standing offers

A 'standing offer' is a purchasing arrangement under which there is no legal obligation on the part of the buyer to make a purchase. To summarise their use, standing offers are frequently employed where the amount of a good or service required is not definitely known. In these circumstances, suppliers are asked to tender their prices against a useage guide from previous years, but no contractual commitment is made to buy any or all of a maximum quantity specified. Within Government, they are misleadingly known by many names by different departments, such as enabling arrangements, demand order contracts, framework arrangements, call-off contracts, and so on. Sometimes they are confused with and are actually referred to as 'call-off contracts'.

In making use of a standing offer, many separate contracts are formed throughout the period in question as the supplier's continuing offer is accepted without qualification. The appropriate Directive only applies when the aggregate value of the individual contracts made under the arrangement exceed the threshold. If there is any likelihood of that value nearing the relevant threshold during the 'contract' period, it is wise to employ one of the EC procurement procedures at the outset. If this is not done, and the value of the individual contracts does reach the threshold in the relevant Directive, all further contracts that would have been made using the standing offer must be advertised. To avoid such an unsatisfactory situation arising, great care should be taken when estimating the eventual value of the contract.

❏ Enforcement of the Directives

The underlying legal basis for the EC Directives is contained in the Treaty of Rome. Government purchasing decisions which violate the Treaty may be challenged in the European Court of Justice by the EC Commission or another Member State.

By implementing the obligations of the Compliance Directive (89/665/EEC) into UK law, aggrieved suppliers and service providers can take action against non-compliant contracting authorities in the courts of the United Kingdom. They may take the form of:

- claims arising from a company's belief that they would have been awarded the contract had the purchasing process been properly conducted
- claims that the *OJEC* advertisement was improperly worded leading to a failure of the company to respond
- claims that the company was improperly excluded from the purchasing process.

Action in the UK concerning the possible breach of Public Contract Regulations is brought in the High Court of England and Wales and in the Court of Session in Scotland. By way of interim measures prior to final trial, these courts have the power to:

- suspend the procedure leading to contract award
- suspend the decision of the contracting authority stemming from the award procedure.

At the final trial, the courts may award damages to the aggrieved supplier if a contract has been entered into improperly.

Both the EC Commission and other Member States have the power to take action in the European Court of Justice against a Member State in breach of the Supplies and Services Directives. This applies where the Commission

> considers that a clear and manifest infringement of the Community provisions in the field of public procurement has been committed ....

Annex A

Description of some standard conditions of Government contracts

SC 1 Interpretations, etc– Standard Condition 1 contains definitions and interpretations of terms used in the standard conditions and in the contract. All contracts should state that the relevant departmental Secretary of State is designated as the Authority for the purpose of the contract.

SC 2 Specifications, etc – Standard Condition 2 underlines the importance of the specification, drawings, etc, in the description of the articles ordered under the contract.

SC 3 Alteration of Specifications, Plans, Drawings, Patterns and Samples – Standard Condition 3 gives the Authority the right to alter the specifications and drawings etc from time to time, and states that, if affected, the contract price or the delivery may be subject to revision.

SC 4 Inspection – Standard Condition 4 contains the general rules on inspection and rejection. More particular inspection requirements are normally included in the contract schedule.

SC 5 Acceptance Marks – Standard Condition 5 provides for the marking of contract Articles, if necessary, with the Government broad arrow or crown. Details of marking may be given in the specification.

SC 6 Packages – Standard Condition 6 expresses the general rule that all containers are non-returnable. Government policy is to pay for and retain containers except gas cylinders, carboys and other specialised containers. If containers are to be returned, this fact should be stated in the contract and appropriate arrangements made.

SC 7 Delivery – Standard Condition 7 is very important. It defines, amongst other things:

- when *property* in the completed Articles moves from the seller to the buyer
- the contractual delivery point, when *risk* moves from the seller to the buyer.

(The Sale of Goods Act (1979) does not refer to the word 'ownership', but speaks instead of either 'property' or 'title'. Lawyers will argue at great length about the meaning of these words, but for most practical purposes, property, ownership and title can be regarded as the same.)

Clause (1) requires the contractor to 'hand over' the completed Articles at the time, place and manner specified in the contract. The term 'delivery' is not used as this implies physical delivery to the Authority eg by rail, road, sea or air transport, which may not always be appropriate. Although most government contracts involve such a form of delivery, many do not require the goods to be delivered in the normal sense but 'handed over', perhaps to another contractor who requires the goods to complete another Government contract, or 'handed over' to a special store on the contractor's premises.

Clause (2) is concerned with the proper packing and securing of the Articles, as specified in the contract; also the contractor's compliance with any additional instructions the Authority may issue concerning transportation of the Articles, subject to an addition to the contract price where necessary.

Clause (3) is concerned with methods of delivery. For example, 'ex-works' ie collected by the purchasing department, free on rail (f.o.r.), free along side (f.a.s.), free on board (f.o.b.) or free delivery to destination (f.d.d.), this last meaning that the contractor is responsible for transport of the Articles and that delivery is paid for within the contract price. Risk for loss or damage in transit will vary, depending upon the point at which contractual delivery takes place. This is considered further under Standard Condition 12, below.

Clause (4) precisely defines the point at which contractual delivery takes place. For 'normal' deliveries, ie those described under Clause (3) above, delivery of the Articles occurs when they go into the possession of the Authority or the Authority's agent.

Clause (5) deals with the passing of property, and the general principle of GC/Stores/1 is that property passes upon delivery, as defined by Clause (4). However, there is an important exception to this general principle. Where stage or progress payments have been incorporated into the contract, the Government's right of ownership is required to be protected by ensuring that the right of ownership passes earlier than on delivery (see SC 49 – Vesting).

Clause (6) is concerned with Articles rejected under SC 24 (Rejection) after inspection under the terms of SC 4 (Inspection). Clause (6) says that rejected Articles will be considered as not being delivered in the contractual sense and that property in the Articles will revert to the contractor.

SC 8 Rendering of Bills – Standard Condition 8 informs the contractor how bills for payment should be submitted. The address of the Bill Paying Authority will be stated in the tender and contract documents.

SC 9 Recovery of Sums Due – Standard Condition 9 gives any central Government department having contracts with the contractor, the right to recover from payment due to the contractor any money the contractor may owe under any Government contract containing SC 9.

The contractor may 'owe' the government money as a result of:

(a) a downward adjustment of a fixed price (see chapter 5, Variation of Price)

(b) damage or loss of property issued to the contractor

(c) a downward adjustment of the price due to a lessening of the specification during the course of the contract

(d) the recovery of the cost of return of rejected Articles, where the contractor has failed to remove them at his own expense (see SC 24 – Rejection)

(e) a claim against the contractor under SC 14 Default, Clause 2, or liquidated damages.

SC 10 Progress Reports – Standard Condition 10 requires the contractor to provide the Authority with contract progress reports 'as may be reason ably called for'. Where such reports are provided and accepted, and a late delivery is forecast, the Authority's rights under SC 14 Default are not prejudiced.

SC 11 Issues of Government Property – Standard Condition 11 deals with the rights of ownership, maintenance, loss and damage of Government property issued to the contractor under the contract. Government property is usually issued when items require repair or modification. The 'Issued Property' in this case may also include replacement parts as well as the actual item requiring repair or modification.

SC 12 Loss of or Damage to the Articles – Standard Condition 12 sets out the contractor's responsibilities in the event of loss or damage. Under Clause (1), the contractor is responsible up to 'delivery' as defined in SC 7 Delivery, and as such is required to make good any loss or damage 'howsoever occasioned'.

Clause (2) of SC 12 brings out the point that the contractor is responsible for loss or damage even if the goods have been inspected by the Authority or even if the property (ownership) has passed to the Authority under SC49 Vesting (see below).

Clause (3) emphasises the point that, generally, the contractor is responsible for the goods up until delivery. However, if an Article is rejected by the Authority after delivery, the contractor again becomes responsible for loss or damage when it is taken back, or if it is not collected by the contractor, after a certain time limit.

SC 13 Value Added Tax – Standard Condition 13 provides for the Authority to pay the contractor, in addition to the contract price, a sum equal to the VAT chargeable on the supply of the goods or services supplied under the contract.

SC 14 Default – If contractors do not meet their contractual obligations, then they are in default. The only aspect of default with which Standard Condition 14 is concerned is the contractor's failure to deliver on time. The rights conferred upon the department under this Condition are:

(a) to terminate the contract in respect of the Articles not delivered by the due date or dates

(b) to purchase these Articles elsewhere

(c) to recover from the defaulting contractor any extra costs incurred under (b).

Under Clause 1, if the contractor fails to complete delivery by the date specified in the contract, the Authority has the power to terminate the contract either in respect of the Articles which are late in delivery, for example, a particular batch, or in respect of all of the items under the contract, even though they may not be due for delivery when termination occurs. If SC14 is invoked by the Authority, the rights and obligations of the parties concerning deliveries made in accordance with the contract are not affected, for example the Authority would be still be obliged to pay the contract price for the Articles properly delivered.

Any action taken by the Authority under SC14 is without prejudice to any other remedies available, and so it would be possible for a department, if it should wish, also to sue for damages suffered as a result of late delivery.

Clause (2) gives the Authority the right, should it so wish, to go elsewhere and purchase the Articles upon which the Contractor has defaulted. In addition, any extra cost incurred by the Authority in purchasing the Articles elsewhere may be charged to the defaulting contractor. The provisions of Standard Condition 9, Recovery of Sums Due, may be used for this purpose.

In practice, the Authority's rights may be lost entirely if:

(a) they are not exercised within a reasonable period of the failure to deliver on time

(b) the Authority allows or encourages the contractor, after being in default of delivery, to continue with the contract with out giving a formal extension of time

(c) the Authority could be held by any other act or failure to act, to have condoned the failure to deliver on time.

A default clause that would be appropriate for a service contract rather than goods is contained in Central Unit on Procurement Guidance Number 42 – Condition 25.

SC 15 Bankruptcy, etc – Standard Condition 15 defines the Authority's power to terminate the contract, without compensation, in the event of the contractor's bankruptcy or if a receiver is appointed. Termination does not affect the Authority's rights of ownership either under SC 49 Vesting or SC 11 Issues of Government Property or any other rights of action concerning of matters that arise before or after the contract is terminated.

SC 16 Racial Discrimination – Standard Condition 16 requires contractors in Great Britain to comply with the provisions of the 1968 Race Relations Act (and the replacement 1976 Act). This Act does not apply to Northern Ireland, but the condition requires contractors in Northern Ireland to ensure that the provisions of the Act apply to subcontractors in other parts of the United Kingdom. This condition stems from statements by Ministers at the time to use the Government's influence as a major purchaser to discourage racial discrimination in employment by withholding contracts from companies in breach of the Act.

SC 17 Fair Wages, etc – Standard Condition 17 gave contractual force to a House of Commons Resolution passed in 1946 concerning payment of fair wages by Government contractors. This Resolution was rescinded by the House of Commons in September 1983 with the result that SC 17 no longer has any validity and ceases to be referred to in Government contracts.

SC 18 Transfer and Sub-letting –The purpose of Standard Condition 18 is to prevent a contractor from entering into a contract with the Authority and then transferring it for completion to a third party. The condition not only relates to the contract but to any 'benefit or advantage', such as Government rights in the use of the design.

Where a contractor is the subject of a take over, the Authority's permission is required for the contract to be assigned to the new contractor. This is done by way of an agreement between the parties using a process called 'novation', whereby the contractual obligations are passed to the new contractor after the original contractor is released.

SC 19 Customs Duty – Drawback – Standard Condition 19 requires the contractor to include within the contract price any UK Customs and Excise or other duty payable on goods imported from outside the EC. In addition, it does not allow the contractor to claim any duty that is refundable should the Articles supplied under the contract be subsequently exported. This condition is therefore not appropriate for contracts for imported defence equipment where import duty may be waived.

SC 20 Corrupt Gifts and Payments of Commission – If a contractor is judged to have given corrupt gifts to any person 'in Her Majesty's Service' as an inducement, either to obtain a contract or as a reward for an associated favour, Standard Condition 20 gives the Authority power to:

    (a) terminate the contract

    (b) recover from the contractor any loss to the Authority arising from the termination

    (c) recover from the contractor the value of any gift, etc

    (d) to act as if there had been a failure in delivery and thereby take purchase in default action under Clause 2 of SC 14 in respect of the Articles ordered under the terminated contract and to charge any extra cost incurred to the contractor.

The utmost probity is required between the contractor and the staff of Government departments, and this powerful condition reflects the severity with which corruption in public service dealings is viewed by Parliament and Government.

SC 21 Official Secrets Act – The purpose of Standard Condition 21 is to emphasise the importance of the Official Secrets Acts by placing the contractor under obligation to ensure that all persons employed on any work in connection with the contract know of the Acts and of their effect. It is important to note that there is no time limit to the statutory provisions and so they continue beyond the conclusion of the contract.

Standard Conditions 22, 22a, 23 and 23a – These conditions existed in earlier editions of GC/Stores/1 but were deleted from the 1979 edition. They became Standard Conditions 29, 29a, 30 and 30a and cover Law and Arbitration (see below).

SC 24 Rejection – Standard Condition 24 (Clause (1)) gives the Authority the right to reject any Article which on inspection under SC 4 does not conform with the contract requirements. Property in rejected Articles reverts to the Contractor on receipt of notice of rejection; SC 7(6) refers.

Clause (2) gives the Authority the added right to reject the whole of any consignment, not just the items inspected.

Clause (3) requires the contractor to remove rejected articles at their own expense within a certain time.

Clause (4) gives the Authority the right to return rejected articles at the contractor's expense, at the contractor's risk (SC 12(3) refers).

Clause (5) requires the contractor to deliver within the contract delivery period, or any extension of it, a replacement for every rejected Article, at the contractor's expense.

Clause (6) covers an appeals procedure and Clause (7) concerns the marking of rejected items.

SC 25 Acceptance –Acceptance is the formal act of agreement by the buyer that the goods comply with the requirements of the contract, as far as it is possible to tell. Once goods have been accepted by the buyer, the right of rejection is lost. Remedies in respect of defects subsequently discovered may be pursued by any other remedies open to the Authority.

SC 25 states that acceptance takes place, when the Authority confirms acceptance in accordance with the contract procedure specified or, in the absence of an acceptance procedure:

(a) when the Article is taken into use, or

(b) when the Article has not been rejected within any time limit occasioned by SC 24, or

(c) after a reasonable time from delivery.

Although the right of rejection is lost once Articles have been accepted, it does not negate the rights of the Authority, under the terms of the contract or elsewhere, to exercise any other remedies open to it should the Articles subsequently prove to be defective.

Standard Conditions 26, 27 and 28 – The 1979 Edition of GC/Stores/1 does not contain any conditions under these numbers, and so this concludes the outline of the conditions contained in Part I of GC/Stores/1; Part II commences with SC 29 and ends with SC 60.

The following (or their equivalents) are the most commonly used conditions from Part II.

SC 29 Law (English); SC 29a Law (Scottish) – It is important that any Government contract stipulates which law is applicable so that there is no dispute should a legal opinion be sought on any contractual matter. These conditions, as appropriate, declare the law governing the contract.

SC 30 Arbitration (English Law) – Unless the contract is of very small value, many Government contracts provide for disputes to be referred to arbitration under the provisions of the Arbitration Act of 1950. For contracts governed by English Law, this is done by including SC 30 in the contract. Its inclusion does not affect either party's right to take court action. Matters upon which the Authority has reserved the right to take the final decision are excluded by this condition from arbitration.

SC 30a Arbitration (Scottish Law) – The Arbitration Act of 1950 does not apply in Scotland. Therefore, where SC 29a applies and the contract is subject to Scottish Law, a different Arbitration condition, in the form of SC 30a, is required. This explains in Clause (2) that the decision of the arbitrators or oversman (umpire) is final, subject to matters of law being referred to the Court of Sessions or, on appeal, to the House of Lords.

SC 31 Use of Documents, Information, etc – Standard Condition 31 requires the contractor to restrict the disclosure of the existence of the contract and to control the use of information supplied to the contractor for the purposes of the contract only. In addition, the contractor is reminded that any samples, patterns or any specifications, plans, drawings or any other documents issued to the contractor remain the property of the Authority and must be returned on completion of the contract.

SC 49 Vesting – It is a principle of Government contracting that goods are generally not paid for until they are delivered. Where, however, it is considered appropriate for the provision of some form of progress or stage payment in the contract (see chapter 8), then Standard Condition 49, or some equivalent, must also be included. The purpose of this condition is to make the property (ie the ownership) of the materials, components, sub-assemblies, etc, vest in the Authority, as they are acquired or allocated for incorporation in the Articles. Similarly, completed Articles not yet delivered are made the property of the Authority. This is particularly important in the case of contractors going into receivership or liquidation, and the condition emphasises in Clause (2) that no other person has any lien on property which vests in the Authority.

Even though SC 49 gives the Authority *ownership*, SC 12 ensures that the *risk* of loss or damage remains with the contractor until delivery.

SC 53 Pricing on Ascertained Costs – Reference to this condition is included here not as an encouragement to use it to price on the basis of cost plus profit as a percentage of costs, the least desirable method of pricing, but because it may be used for any form of cost-based pricing, such as cost plus fixed fee, target cost incentive, etc (see chapter 5).

It is a complicated condition, although, in essence, it describes precisely what the Authority will pay, that is, 'the costs properly incurred for the purposes of the Contract', comprising:

- 'wages and salaries constituting a direct charge'
- 'costs in respect of the provision of jigs and tools'
- 'overhead and administration charges appropriate to the Contract'
- 'a sum for profit to be agreed in accordance with the Government Profit Formula' (see chapter 9).

SC 56 Break – Apart from SC56, there are five other Standard Conditions in GC/Stores/1 which allow the Authority to terminate the contract. These are:

SC14 – Default
SC15 – Bankruptcy, etc
SC20 – Corrupt Gifts and Payments of Commission
SC36 – Labour Conditions (Made-up Textiles, Equipment, etc)
SC59 – Security measures.

These five provide for termination in the case of a specific breach of contract. However, Standard Condition 56 allows the Authority to terminate the contract at any time, for any reason whatsoever, by giving written notice to the contractor. It would be usual to include such a condition in contracts of sufficient value or long period of duration to make it worthwhile.

The circumstances which may necessitate the use of this condition are typically those resulting from a change in Government social, economic, defence or foreign policy, such that the need for the contract requirement is affected. Existing contracts, under which part or whole deliveries have yet to be made, need to be terminated using SC 56 if the Articles are no longer required. This is assuming, of course, that it is more economic to terminate than to let the contract run its course.

The contractor's rights under this condition, if termination takes place, are essentially that the Authority will pay a fair and reasonable price for:

> all unused and undamaged materials, bought-out parts and
> components and articles in course of manufacture,

and indemnify the Contractor against:

> any commitments, liabilities or expenditure which are reasonably and
> properly chargeable by the Contractor.

It should be noted that the contractor has no right to terminate under any of the conditions in GC/Stores/1. Although it may just be possible to concede that the contractor might be given the right to terminate a long duration service contract *subject to mutual agreement only*, it is surprising to see the number of 'home grown' conditions which include rights similar to SC 56 for the contractor!

Reference

Central Unit on Procurement (1993) *Contracting for Provision of Services* London, Central Unit on Procurement

Annex B

Contents of Contract and Tender Notices

❏ Item 1

Contents of Contract Notice, Open Procedure, Supplies

1   **Awarding authority:** Name, address and telephone, telegraphic, telex and facsimile numbers of the contracting authority.

2   **(a)**   **The award procedure chosen:** eg Open Procedure.

    (b)   **Contract type:** eg Purchase, Framework Agreement, Call-Off Contract, etc.

3   **(a)**   **Place of delivery:** Consignee.

    (b)   **Goods:** Nature and quantity of the goods to be supplied.

    (c)   **Division into lots:** An indication of whether the suppliers can tender for some and/or all of the goods required.

    (d)   **Derogation from Art.8(2):** Derogation from the use of standards in accordance with Article 8(2) eg 'no'.

4   **Delivery deadline:** Date

5   **(a)**   **Documents from:** Name and address from which tender documents may be requested.

    (b)   **Requests not later than:** Final date for such requests.

    (c)   **Fee:** The amount and terms of payment of any sum payable for such documents.

6   **(a)**   **Deadline for receipt of tenders:**

    (b)   **Address:** Address to which tenders must be sent.

    (c)   **Language(s):** Language or languages in which tenders must be completed.

7   **(a)**   **Opening of tenders (persons admitted):** The persons authorised to be present at the opening of tenders.

    (b)   **Date, time and place:** Date, time and place of tender opening.

8.   **Deposits and guarantees:** The deposits and guarantees required eg indemnity insurance, if appropriate.

9   **Financing and payment:** The main terms concerning financing and payment and/or references to the relevant provisions eg 'see tender documents'.

10   **Legal form in case of group bidders:** The legal form to be taken by a grouping of suppliers winning the contract eg 'no special legal form required but each supplier to become jointly and severally responsible for the contract before acceptance'.

11   **Qualifications:** The information and formalities necessary for an appraisal of the minimum economic and technical standards of the supplier.

12   **Tenders may lapse after:** Period for which the tenderer is required to keep the tender open.

13   **Award criteria (other than price):** For example, the most economically advantageous tender, with award criteria following in order of preference.

14   **Other information:** eg address for technical queries, or, if not covered in tender documents, a statement that completed tenders shall be priced in sterling, and that the contract shall be considered as a contract made in England (Scotland) and according to English (Scottish) Law and subject to the exclusive jurisdiction of the English (Scottish) Courts.

15   **Notice postmarked:** Date of despatch of the Notice.

16   **Notice received on:** Date of receipt by the Office for Official Publications of the European Communities.

❏ Item 2

Contents of Tender Notice, Open Procedure, Services

1   **Awarding authority:** Name, address and telephone, telegraphic, telex and facsimile numbers of the contracting authority.

2   **Category of service and description, CPC reference number:**

3   **Delivery to:** Consignee.

4   **(a)**   **Reserved for a particular profession:** An indication of whether the execution of the service is reserved by law, regulation or administration provision to a particular profession.

    (b)   **Reference to the law, regulation or administration provision.**

    (c)   **Names of and qualifications of personnel:** An indication of whether legal persons should indicate the names and professional qualifications of the staff to be responsible for the execution of the service.

5   **Division into lots:** An indication as to whether service providers may tender for part of the services required.

6   **Variants:** Where applicable, non-acceptance of variants.

7   **Duration of contract or time limit for completion of the service:** Period or date as appropriate.

8   **(a)**   **Documents from:** Name and address from which tender documents may be requested.

    (b)   **Requests not later than:** Final date for such requests.

    (c)   **Fee:** The amount and terms of payment of any sum payable for such documents.

9   **(a)**   **Opening of tenders (persons admitted):** The persons authorised to be present at the opening of tenders.

    (b)   **Date, time and place:** Date, time and place of opening tenders.

10   **Deposits and guarantees:** The deposits and guarantees required eg indemnity insurance, if appropriate.

11   **Financing and payment:** The main terms concerning financing and payment and/or references to the relevant provisions.

12   **Legal form in case of group bidders:** The legal form to be taken by a grouping of suppliers winning the contract.

13. **Qualifications:** The information and formalities necessary for an appraisal of the minimum economic and technical standards of the service provider.

14 **Tenders may lapse after:** Period for which the tenderer is required to keep the tender open.

15 **Award criteria (other than price):** For example, the most economically advantageous tender, with award criteria following in order of preference.

16 **Other information:** eg address for technical queries, or, if not covered in tender documents, a statement that completed tenders shall be priced in sterling, and that the contract shall be considered as a contract made in England (Scotland) and according to English (Scottish) Law and subject to the exclusive jurisdiction of the English (Scottish) Courts.

17 **Notice postmarked:** The date of despatch of the Notice.

18 **Notice received on:** The date Notice received by the Office for Official Publications of the European Communities.

❑ Item 3

Contents of Contract Notice , Restricted Procedure, Supplies

1   **Awarding authority:** Name, address and telephone, telegraphic, telex and facsimile numbers of the contracting authority.

2   **(a)   Award procedure:** eg Restricted Procedure.

    (b)   Justification for accelerated procedure: eg 'urgent operational requirement', if appropriate.

    (c)   Contract type: eg Purchase, Framework Agreement, Call-Off Contract, etc.

3   **(a)   Delivery to:** Consignee.

    (b)   Goods: Nature and quantity of goods to be supplied.

    (c)   Division into lots: An indication of whether the suppliers can tender for some and/or all of the goods required.

    (d)   Derogation from Art. 8(2): Derogation from the use of standards in accordance with Article 8(2) eg 'no'.

4   **Delivery deadline:** Date or 'tenderer to state best delivery offer'.

5   **Legal form in case of group bidders:** The legal form to be taken by a grouping of suppliers winning the contract eg 'no special legal form required but each supplier will be required to become jointly and severally responsible for the contract before acceptance'.

6   **(a)   Deadline for receipt of applications:** Deadline for requests to participate, which must not be less than 37 calendar days from the date of despatch of the Notice or, for the Restricted Accelerated Procedure (see below), not less than 15 calendar days.

    (b)   Address: Address to which applications must be sent.

    (c)   Language(s): Language or languages in which applications must be drawn up.

7   **Final date for the despatch of invitations to tender:** 'Applicants who have not been notified by this date should assume that they have not been invited to tender'.

8   **Qualifications:** The information and formalities necessary for an appraisal of the minimum economic and technical standards of the supplier.

9   **Award criteria (other than price):** For example, 'the most economically advantageous tender', with award criteria following in order of preference.

10 **Other information:** For example, an address for technical queries, or, if not covered in tender documents, a statement that completed tenders shall be priced in sterling, and that the contract shall be considered as a contract made in England (Scotland) and according to English (Scottish) Law and subject to the exclusive jurisdiction of the English (Scottish) Courts.

11 **Notice postmarked:** Date of despatch of Notice.

12 **Notice received on:** The date of receipt by the Office for Official Publications of the European Communities.

❏ Item 4

Contents of Tender Notice, Restricted Procedure, Services

1   **Awarding authority:** Name, address and telephone, telegraphic, telex and facsimile numbers of the contracting authority.

2   **Category of service and description, CPC reference number:**

3   **Delivery to:** Consignee.

4   (a)   **Reserved for a particular profession:** An indication of whether the execution of the service is reserved by law, regulation or administration provision to a particular profession.

    (b)   **Law, regulation or administrative provision:**

    (c)   **Names of and qualifications of personnel:** An indication of whether legal persons should indicate the names and professional qualifications of the staff to be responsible for the execution of the service.

5   **Division into lots:** An indication as to whether service providers may tender for part of the services required.

6   **Number of service providers which will be invited to tender:** Envisaged number or range of service providers which will be invited to tender. If this option is completed, the range must cover from 5 to 20 providers.

7   **Variants:** Where applicable, non-acceptance of variants.

8   **Duration of contract or time limit for completion of the service:** Period or date as appropriate.

9   **Legal form in case of group bidders:** The legal form to be taken by a grouping of suppliers winning the contract.

10   (a)   **Justification for accelerated procedure:**

    (b)   **Deadline for receipt of applications:** Deadline for requests to participate, which must not be less than 37 calendar days from the date of despatch of the Notice or, for the Accelerated Restricted Procedure (see below), not less than 15 calendar days.

    (c)   **Address:** Address to which applications to particpate must be sent.

    (d)   **Language(s):** Language or languages in which applications must be drawn up.

11   **Final date for the despatch of invitations to tender:**

12   **Deposits and guarantees:** The deposits and guarantees required eg indemnity insurance, if appropriate.

13   **Qualifications:** The information and formalities necessary for an appraisal of the minimum economic and technical standards of the service provider.

14   **Award criteria (other than price):** For example, the most economically advantageous tender, with award criteria following in order of preference.

15   **Other information:** eg address for technical queries, or, if not covered in tender documents, a statement that completed tenders shall be priced in sterling, and that the contract shall be considered as a contract made in England (Scotland) and according to English (Scottish) Law and subject to the exclusive jurisdiction of the English (Scottish) Courts.

16   **Notice postmarked:** The date of despatch of the Notice.

17   **Notice received on:** The date Notice received by the Office for Official Publications of the European Communities.

❑ Item 5

Contents of Tender Notice , Negotiated Procedure, Supplies

1   **Awarding authority:** Name, address and telephone, telegraphic, telex and facsimile numbers of the contracting authority.

2   **(a)**   **Award procedure:** eg Negotiated Procedure.

     (b)   **Justification for accelerated procedure:** eg 'urgent operational requirement', if appropriate.

     (c)   **Contract type:** eg Purchase, Framework Agreement, Call-Off Contract, etc.

3   **(a)**   **Delivery to:** Consignee.

     (b)   **Goods:** Nature and quantity of goods to be supplied.

     (c)   **Division into lots:** An indication of whether the suppliers can tender for some and/or all of the goods required.

     (d)   **Derogation from Art. 8(2):** Derogation from the use of standards in accordance with Article 8(2) eg 'no'.

4   **Delivery deadline:** Date or 'tenderer to state best delivery offer'.

5   **Legal form in case of group bidders:** The legal form to be taken by a grouping of suppliers winning the contract eg 'no special legal form required but each supplier will be required to become jointly and severally responsible for the contract before acceptance'.

6   **(a)**   **Deadline for receipt of applications:** Deadline for requests to participate, which must not be less than 37 calendar days from the date of despatch of the Notice or, for the Accelerated Negotiated Procedure (see below), not less than 15 calendar days.

     (b)   **Address:** Address to which applications must be sent.

     (c)   **Language(s):** Language or languages in which applications must be drawn up.

7   **Final date for the despatch of invitations to tender:** 'Applicants who have not been notified by this date should assume that they have not been invited to tender'.

8   **Qualifications:** The information and formalities necessary for an appraisal of the minimum economic and technical standards of the supplier.

9   **Award criteria (other than price):** For example, 'the most economically advantageous tender', with award criteria following in order of preference.

10 **Other information:** For example, an address for technical queries, or, if not covered in tender documents, a statement that completed tenders shall be priced in sterling, and that the contract shall be considered as a contract made in England (Scotland) and according to English (Scottish) Law and subject to the exclusive jurisdiction of the English (Scottish) Courts.

11 **Notice postmarked:** Date of despatch of Notice.

12 **Notice received on:** The date of receipt by the Office for Official Publications of the European Communities.

❑ Item 6

Contents of Tender Notice, Negotiated Procedure, Services

1   **Awarding authority:** Name, address and telephone, telegraphic, telex and facsimile numbers of the contracting authority.

2   **Category of service and description, CPC reference number:**

3   **Delivery to:** Consignee.

4   **(a)   Reserved for a particular profession:** An indication of whether the execution of the service is reserved by law, regulation or administration provision to a particular profession.

    (b)   Law, regulation or administrative provision:

    (c)   Names of and qualifications of personnel: An indication of whether legal persons should indicate the names and professional qualifications of the staff to be responsible for the execution of the service.

5   **Division into lots:** An indication as to whether service providers may tender for part of the services required.

6   **Number of service providers which will be invited to tender:** Envisaged number or range of service providers which will be invited to tender. If this option is completed, the range must cover from 5 to 20 providers.

7   **Variants:** Where applicable, non-acceptance of variants.

8   **Duration of contract or time limit for completion of the service:** Period or date as appropriate.

9   **Legal form in case of group bidders:** The legal form to be taken by a grouping of suppliers winning the contract.

10   **(a)   Justification for accelerated procedure:**

    (b)   Deadline for receipt of applications: Deadline for requests to participate, which must not be less than 37 calendar days from the date of despatch of the Notice or, for the Accelerated Negotiated Procedure (see below), not less than 15 calendar days.

    (c)   Address: Address to which applications to participate must be sent.

    (d)   Language(s): Language or languages in which applications must be drawn up.

11 **Deposits and guarantees:** The deposits and guarantees required eg indemnity insurance, if appropriate.

12 **Qualifications:** The information and formalities necessary for an appraisal of the minimum economic and technical standards of the service provider.

13 **Providers already selected:** Where applicable, the names and addresses of service providers already selected by the contracting authority.

14 **Other information:** eg address for technical queries, or, if not covered in tender documents, a statement that completed tenders shall be priced in sterling, and that the contract shall be considered as a contract made in England (Scotland) and according to English (Scottish) Law and subject to the exclusive jurisdiction of the English (Scottish) Courts.

15 **Notice postmarked:** The date of despatch of the Notice.

16 **Notice received on:** The date Notice received by the Office for Official Publications of the European Communities.

17 **Previous date(s) of publication:** The previous publication dates of earlier Notices in the *Official Journal*.

Index